# Lost in the Antebellum

# Lost in the Antebellum

By

Robert D. Morritt

**Cambridge Scholars** Publishing

Lost in the Antebellum

By Robert D. Morritt

This book first published 2011. The present binding first published 2017.

Cambridge Scholars Publishing

Lady Stephenson Library, Newcastle upon Tyne, NE6 2PA, UK

British Library Cataloguing in Publication Data
A catalogue record for this book is available from the British Library



ISBN (10): 1-4438-7972-X
ISBN (13): 978-1-4438-7972-9

The North Carolina residence of J. Grist, Esq., *Harper's New Monthly Magazine*, No.LXXXIV – May 1857 –Vol., XIV – page 751.

*A compendium of the lives of Authors, Poets, Musicians, Scientists and Military exploration within the Antebellum era.*

After American independence and prior to the Civil War, occurred the growth of a new spirit.

The addition of new territories, formerly owned by France and Spain, led to the movement of population westward creating a new Nation, which resulted in a revived America that carried with it a revived national spirit, one of creative enthusiasm .It rose like a Phoenix. It was a time of enthusiasm in a new Nation with high hopes, only to be crushed by the collapse of this society by the advent of the American Civil War. A travel back in time affording the reader a clearer understanding of often overlooked era.

# TABLE OF CONTENTS

# FOREWORD

This compendium of information describes from contemporary sources a variety of people, who contributed directly to the development of this period. Here then are the writers, musicians, frontiersmen abolitionists, explorers, military exploits that occurred during the Antebellum era.

## Background

Included are accounts of;

The diary of an enemy combatant found in recent years, giving a contemporary account of the death of 'Davy Crockett' at the Alamo.

An observation on how the Gulf Stream 'works, by an early American Oceanographer.

A Family of singers who were at the forefront of the abolishment movement.

The 'Old South' with accounts from both sides of 'issues' presented by opposing contemporary authors,

A 'trip' to the Moon (and back) in June 1844

A major composer who heard his major selling song played in the streets when he was penniless.

The invasion of a Central American country by an American filibuster who became the President of Nicaragua for a year.

# PREFACE

## The Participants

Matthew Maury – early oceanographer 'The Gulf Stream

William Gilmore Simms – Author, Poet and Journalist

Mary E.Hewitt – The Poetess

The Hutchinson Family Singers.of New Hampshire. Their travels in England in 1845. Their songs that addressed abolishment and temperance issues of the time.

David "Davy" Crockett, A true account of his life (and death).killed at the Battle of the Alamo.

Six Day in the Moon; Appeared in the *Southern Literary Messenger* – June 1844. Written by an '*Aerio-Nautical Man', who states that he has "just returned from the Moon!"*

Louis Godey – The founder of 'The Ladies Book' 1830, later known as 'Godey's Ladies Book'

John Howard Payne – Composer of the words to "Home, Sweet Home" who recalled hearing his song played in the streets in Europe by organ grinders *when he was penniless.*

Zebulon Pike – Early effort to explore the western Great Plains and Rocky Mountains in Colorado. His capture by the Spanish who paraded him and his fellow explorers through El Paso.

Sara Payson Willis Parton - also known as "Fanny Fern" Writer 1811-1872.

Henry Timrod – The Poet Laureate of the Confederacy

William Walker – Invader of Sonora and Nicaragua, became the President of Nicaragua for one year. His mission to obtain territories for the use of slaves. If he succeeded to add the areas (in Mexico) as additional States within the Union.

James Bowie – Died at the Battle of the Alamo. The controversy of who invented the Bowie knife.

Margaret Fuller – Journalist, critic and women's rights activist associated with the American transcendental movement. She was the first full-time female book reviewer in journalism

Sarah Josepha Hale – Self educated author of 'Mary Had a Little Lamb,who later becane Editor of 'Godey's Ladys Book'

Alice and Phoebe Cary – The 'Sister' Poets from Ohio.

James Howard – Steamboat builder (Built the 'Glendy Burke" the song composed by Stephen Foster.

Stephen Collins Foster – Did he ever visit the mansion at 'Federal Hill' that is alleged to be the home portrayed in his song, "My Old Kentucky Home"?

Harriet Beecher Stowe – "Uncle Tom's Cabin" of which when Abraham Lincoln when he met Stowe at the start of the Civil War, he was quoted as saying "So this is the little lady who made this big war." Both the northern and southern reaction to novel is examined with together with 'rebuttal' novels written by southern authors.

Henry Clay Lewis – The Swamp Doctor

Edgar Allen Poe – His first *published work,* "Tamerlane"published in 1827 of which only only twelve copies are believed to exist.

Lydia Sigourney – Her writings were characterized by fluency, grace and reflection on nature and of a sentimental nature.tHer most successful poems are 'Niagara' and 'Indian Names.'

Caroline Lee Hentz – Author of the pro-slavery novel, “The Planter’s Northern Bride’ her rebuttal to “Uncle Tom’s Cabin”, Hentz extolls the joys of slavery in the Old South.

Sarah Bolton – Poet and early settler in Indiana.

# MATTHEW MAURY

**Born 1806 – Died 1873**

**Founder of the U.S. Naval Observatory**

His books on Navigation show the best sea routes based upon the Winds and currents. Maury later became a Confederate Spy in Europe noted for his work, 'Paper on the Gulf Stream and Currents of the Sea', read before the National Institute, April 2. 1844. His premise was that with "a correct knowledge of the force and set of currents on the ocean" depended "the safety of the vessel and cargo, but the lives of all on board".

At the time of his presentation extremely little was known about Ocean currents. His basis was that seafarers should have a better understanding of currents. He noted that they varied in aspects some were cooler or warmer than the temperature of the sea a craft would navigate through. Maury noted there was a current of cold water running towards the South which had such strength that its pressure affected the topography of the coastline.

## The Gulf Stream

Sir Frances Drake with his fleet, c 1594, had entered Albemarle Sound through the Roanoke inlet, which in the year 1844 had become a sand bank well-above the reach of the highest tides. He cited that in the year 1774 (approximately) it was at that time navigable by vessels "drawing 12 feet of water".

He gave a more in depth description of the effect such as, "A comparison of present charts (year 1841) with Jeffery's atlas published in 1775, shows not only that these shoals are increasing, but the chain of islands alluded to is in the process of gradual formation

He mentioned that Currituck and Roanoke inlets, that once were navigable "are now sand bars", also that "Ocracoke inlet had 17 feet of water, it now has only 8 feet, and Beaufort, North Carolina and Charleston, South Carolina, are now silted up and have become dry land."

He pondered where the source of the sand had come from that formed the islands. He surmised that separated from the main land by standing pools of water moved only by the tides of the Ocean. It could not be brought from the shore. The only way it could form was by being up-heaved within the general elevation of the coast geologically, or it could be formed by being cast up from the bottom of the Ocean by the Gulf Stream and the waves or brought down from the North by the current on the coast. Only investigation could solve this paradox.

After taking in mind geological aspects he further surmised that the source of the coastal current (at that time) was a "matter of conjecture, and its cause a mystery." At this point in time, nautical books had no observations recorded on the cause of the strength or the fluctuation of these currents.

Maury explained that if a vessel proceeded further out into the Atlantic. The ship would find "A vast stream of water running counter to this." It was known as the Gulf Stream bound from the Straits of Florida to the Banks of Newfoundland and thence to the shores of Europe

"Further," he mentioned, "What is its breadth or depth? We are told indeed that even at the same place it runs sometimes at the rate of two knots the hour, sometimes at five, and we know that it may always be found within certain broad limits, varying at the same place, from 140 to 340 miles. with this our knowledge ends; though more accurate information as to it and its offsets would many a time have saved a mariner from disaster and his vessel from shipwreck, and even now, would add more in achieving a speedy and safe navigation of the Atlantic.

Maury noted that Navigators had been in the habit of crossing and re-crossing the Atlantic almost daily for a period (then) of three hundred years. "It's existence". The Gulf Stream[1] even then was not generally known to them., until after Dr. Franklin discovered ***the warmth of its waters*** about 70 years ago (c.1774) and to this day (1844) the information that he gave us constitutes the basis, I had almost said the sum and substance of all we know about it.

When Dr. Franklin was in London in 1770, he was consulted as to a memorial which the Board of Customs at Boston sent to the Lords of the treasury, stating that the Falmouth packets were generally a fortnight[2] longer to New York than common traders were from London to Providence, Rhode Island, they therefore asked that the Falmouth packets sent to Providence instead of New York. This appeared strange to Dr. Franklin as London was much farther than Falmouth, and from Falmouth the routes were the same, and the difference should have been the other way.

He however consulted a Nantucket whaler who chanced to be in London also; the fisherman explained to him that the difference arose from the circumstances that the Rhode Island Captains were acquainted with the Gulf Stream, while those of the English packets were not .The latter kept in it and were set back 60 or 70 miles a day while the former avoided it all together. He had been acquainted with it by the whales which were found on either side of it, but never in it.

At the request of the doctor[3] he then traced on a chart, the course of this stream from the Straits of Florida. The doctor had it engraved at Tower Hill and sent copies of it to the Falmouth Captains, who paid no attention to it. The course of the Gulf Stream as laid down by that fisherman from his general recollection of it, is retained "on our charts at the present day (1844), almost without an alteration."

[1] The Gulf Stream passes northwards from the equator to Britain and without it's presence Britain would have a climate similar to Greenland or Labrador than the one we are more familiar with.

[2] A fortnight is a period of two weeks.

[3] 'Doctor' is Benjamin Franklin.

## Dangers of Winter Voyages

In Dr. Franklin's time, the navigator ***guessed*** as much as he ***calculated*** the place of his ship-vessels from Europe to Boston frequently made New York, and thought the land-fall by no means bad. Chronometers, now so accurate, were then an experiment.

The Nautical Ephemeris itself was faulty and gave errors of thirty miles in the longitude. The instruments of navigation erred by ***degrees*** quite as much as they do now in ***minutes***; for the crude 'cross staff'[4] and 'back staff', the "sea ring" and "mariner's bow", had not yet given place to the nicer sextant and circle of reflection of the present day. Instances are numerous of vessels navigating the Atlantic in those times being 6 degrees, 8 degrees and even ten degrees of longitude out of their reckoning in as many days from port. Our means, therefore, of properly conducting a system of observations upon the currents of the sea, and for following up the investigations of Franklin are much more ample and complete than they have ever been with navigators before.

No part of this world affords a more difficult or dangerous navigation than the approach of our Northern coast in winter. Before the warmth of the Gulf Stream was known, a voyage at this season from Europe to New England, New York and even to the Capes of Delaware or Chesapeake was many times more trying, difficult and dangerous, than it now is. In making this part of the coast, vessels are frequently met by snow storms and gales which mock the seaman's strength and set naught his skill. In a little while, his bark becomes a mass of ice; with her crew frosted and helpless, she remains obedient only to her helm, and is kept away from the Gulf Stream. After a few hours' run, she reaches its edge, and almost at the next bound, passes from the midst of winter into a sea of summer heat.

---

[4] The cross-staff, John Dee introduced it to England in the 1550s. In the improved versions, the rod was graduated directly in degrees. The cross-staff was difficult to use.To obtain consistent results, the observer had to position the end of the pole precisely against his cheek. He had to observe the horizon and a star in two different directions ***while not moving the instrument*** when he ***shifted his gaze from one to the other***. In addition, observations of the sun required the navigator to look directly at the sun. This could be a painful exercise and made it difficult to obtain an accurate altitude for the sun. Later mariners mounted smoked-glass to the ends of the transoms to reduce the glare of the sun.

The ice disappears-the sailor bathes his stiffened limbs in tepid waters; feeling himself invigorated and refreshed with the genial warmth about him, he realizes out there at sea, the fable of Antaeus and his mother Earth. He attempts to make his port again, and is again as rudely met from the North West; but each time he is driven off from the contest-he comes forth from this stream like the ancient son of Neptune, stronger and stronger, until, after many days, his freshened strength prevails, and he at last enters his haven in safety.

I might name instances, for they are not uncommon in which vessels bound to Norfolk or Baltimore with their crews enervated in tropical climates, have encountered, as far down as the Capes of Virginia, snow storms, that have driven them back into the Gulf Stream time and again, and have kept them out for 40, 50.even 60 days, trying to make an anchorage. The number of shipwrecks that occurred on our coast during one month in the winter of '41 (1841), amounted to not less than three a day. How many were saved by seeking refuge with their frosted and disabled crews in the warm waters of the Gulf Stream is a matter of conjecture.

Before their temperature was known, vessels thus distressed, knew of no place of refuge short of the West Indies; and the newspapers of that day,-Franklin's Pennsylvania Gazette among them, inform us that it was no uncommon occurrence for vessels, bound for the Capes of Delaware in winter, to be blown off and to go to the West Indies, and there wait for the return of spring before they would attempt another approach to this part of the coast. Accordingly, Dr. Franklin's[5] discovery of the Gulf Stream temperature was looked upon as one of great importance, not only on account of its affording to the frosted mariner in Winter a convenient refuge from the snow storm, but because of its serving the Navigator with an excellent land mark or beacon for our coast in all weathers and so viewing it, the Doctor ***concealed*** the discovery ***for we were at war*** with England.

When his work on '***Thermometrical Navigation***' appeared, Commodore Troxton wrote to him; "Your publication will be of use to Navigation by rendering sea voyages secure far beyond what even you yourself will immediately calculate, for I have proved the utility of the thermometer very often since we sailed together."

---

[5] Benjamin Franklin.

It will be found a most valuable instrument in the hands of mariners, and particularly as to those who are unacquainted with astronomical observations; these particularly stand in need of a simple method of ascertaining their approach to or distance from the coast, especially in the winter season; for it is then that passages are often prolonged, and the ships blown off the coast by hard westerly winds, and vessels get into the Gulf Stream without its being known; on which account they are often hove to by the Captains supposing themselves near the coast, when they are very far off, (having been drifted by the currents.) On the other hand, ships are often cast on the coast, by sailing in the eddy of the stream, which causes them to outrun their common reckoning. Every year produces new proofs of these facts, and of the calamities incident thereto. Though the warm temperatures of the Gulf Stream were discovered in 1775, yet, for political reasons, the discovery was not generally made known 'till 1790. Its immediate effect was to make the ports of the North as accessible in winter as in summer. Due to its discovery the average passage from Europe to the North was shortened nearly one half.

The place of embouchure for the Gulf Stream is about the latitudinal limits of the Trade winds, where calms and variables prevail; and where aid from currents is most desirable. Our West India Cruisers are continually passing up and down this part of the stream; a few turns to and fro across it, by them, would show how the thread of the current does lie, of which we are now ignorant. It might materially shorten the passage of vessels bound north from the Gulf. The Gulf Stream, as it issues from the straits of Florida, is of a dark indigo blue; the line of junction between it and the green water of the Atlantic, it is plainly seen for hundreds of miles. Though this line is finally lost to the eye as the stream goes north, it is preserved to the thermometer for several thousand miles, yet to this day the limits of the Gulf Stream, even in the most frequented parts of the ocean, though so plainly marked, are but vaguely described on our charts.

Thousands of vessels cross it every year; many of them make observations upon it, and many more, if invited would do the same. The most generally received opinion, however is the one repeated by Dr. Franklin, that the Gulf Stream is the escaping of the waters that have been ***forced*** into the Caribbean Sea by the Trade winds; and that it is the pressure of those winds upon the water, which forces up into that Sea ahead, as it were for this stream. Major Rennell likens the stream to "an immense river descending from a higher level into a plain." Now we know very nearly the average breadth and velocity of the Gulf Stream in the Florida pass.

We also know with a like degree of approximation, the velocity and breadth of the same waters off Cape Hatteras. Their breadth here is about 75 miles against 32 in the "Narrows of the Straits", and their mean velocity is 3 knots off Hatteras against 4 in the "Narrows". This being the case, it is easy to show that the depth of the Gulf Stream off Hatteras is not so great as it is in the "Narrows" of Bimini by nearly 50 per cent, and that consequently, instead of ***descending***, its bed represents the surface of an inclined plain from the North, ***up*** *w*hich the lower depths of the stream ***must*** ascend. If we assume its depth off Bimini to be 200 fathoms, which are thought to be within limits, the above rates of breadth and velocity will give 114 fathoms for its depth off Hatteras. The waters therefore in the straits are below the level of the Hatteras depth, so far from descending. Are actually forced up an inclined plane, whose submarine ascent is not less than 10 inches to the mile!

Moreover, while the Gulf Stream is running to the North from its supposed elevated level at the South, there is a cold current coming down from the North; meeting the warm waters of the Gulf midway the Ocean, it divides itself and runs by the side of them right back into those very reservoirs at the South, to which theory gives an elevation sufficient to send out entirely across the Atlantic a jet of warm water said to be more than three thousand times greater in volume than the Mississippi river.

This current from Baffin's Bay has not only no trade winds to give it a head; but the prevailing winds are unfavorable to it, and for a great part of the way it is below the surface, and far beyond the propelling reach of any wind and there is every reason to believe that this polar current is quite equal in volume to the Gulf Stream.

We know not what the depth or the under temperature of the Gulf Stream may be, but assuming the temperature and velocity at the depth of 200 fathoms, to be those of the surface (which is probably not the case.) and taking the well-known difference between the capacity of air and of water for specific heat, as the arguments, a simple calculation will show, that the quantity of heat discharged over the Atlantic from the waters of the Gulf Stream in a winter's day, would be sufficient to raise the whole column of atmosphere that rests upon France and the British Islands, from the freezing point to summer heat.

In a valuable paper on currents[6] Mr.Redfield states, that in '31, the harbor of St. John's, Newfoundland was closed with ice as late as the month of June; yet who ever heard of the port of Liverpool, on the other side, though 2 degrees *further North being* closed with ice, even in the dead of winter? In whatever may tend to the improvement of Navigation, or redound to the credit of their country, the officers of the Navy have always been ready. Any plan for collecting facts and systematizing observations in the fields proposed, is sure to receive from them the most zealous and hearty co-operation, when it does not interfere with their more immediate duties. The commercial marine of no country in the world can boast of ship masters superior to the Americans as Navigators and in general intelligence.

Their industry and enterprise warrant the expectation that they too would join hands in the undertaking most readily. Personal knowledge of them warrants the belief, that at the invitation of the Institute they would undertake a series of observations upon any plan the society may propose.

Excerpts from; 'Paper on the Gulf Stream and Currents of the Sea' read before the National Institute, April 2nd, 1844) by M. F. Maury, Lt., U.S.N.

---

[6] American Journal of Science, Vol.45, p.293.

# WILLIAM GILMORE SIMMS

Simms was born on April 17, 1806, in Charleston, South Carolina. His mother died when he was a young child. His grandmother basically reared him as his father, after experiencing a failed business, left the family home and signed up with Coffee's Indian fighters. Simms was brought up by his grandmother. He started to write poetry whilst still at Grade School. Then, still in his youth, he worked as a clerk in a drug store and decided to study law.

Later he married Anne Giles (1826). He started prectising law a year later but then decided to become an Author instead. When he was nineteen he wrote a dedication to General Charles Cotesworth Pinckney. In 1827 he wrote ***Lyrical and Other Poems and Early Lays***. In 1828 he became a journalist as well as editor and part owner of the ***City Gazette***, a role he held until 1832 when the publication failed. Simms then devoted his attention entirely to writing and published ***Tile Vision of Cones, Cain, and Other Poems*** (1829); ***The Tricolor, or Three Days of Blood in Paris*** (1830); and his strongest poem, ***Atalantis, a Tale of the Sea*** (1832). ***Atalantis*** established him as an author. His novel *Martin* ***Faber, the Story of a Criminal***, was published in 1833 and madehim known to a wider audience.

He was known amongst literary circles as a prominent part of Antebellum literature He is was also remembered for his strong support of slavery and his opposition to ***Uncle Tom's Cabin***, in response to which he wrote reviews and a novel. Edgar Allan Poe pronounced him the best novelist America had ever produced.

In recent decades, Simms was one of the most highly respected, historians of his day. His ***History of South Carolina*** (1842) became the standard school textbook on the state's history. He also wrote popular biographies of Revolutionary War heroes Francis Marion, Nathanael Greene, and John Laurens, as well as John Smith and the Chevalier Bayard. He also became a popular lecturer on American history and accumulated one of the largest collections of Revolutionary War manuscripts, which sadly were lost. Sherman's army burned his home.

In Simms' later years, he became part of the Southern plantation class and firmly supported slavery and Southern secession. During the American Civil War Simms espoused the side of the Secessionists in a weekly newspaper. He served in the state House of Representatives in 1844–1846, after which he was defeated in the election for lieutenant-governor by only one vote. The University of Alabama conferred on him the degree of LLD, He died at his home at 13 Society Street in Charleston on June 11, 1870; he is buried in Magnolia Cemetery.

## Poems and Sonnets

**VIII BYRON**
For Byron's home and fame,
It needed manhood only! Had he known
How sorrow should be borne, nor sunk in shame,
For that his destiny decreed to moan—
His muse had been triumphant over Time
As still she is o'er Passion: still sublime—
Having subdued her soul's infirmity
To aliment; and, with herself o'ercome,
O'ercome the barriers of Eternity,
And lived through all the ages; with a sway
Complete, and unembarrass'd by the doom
That makes of Nature's porcelain common clay!

**THE EDGE OF THE SWAMP**
'Tis a wild spot, and even in summer hours,
With wondrous wealth of beauty and a charm
For the sad fancy, hath the gloomiest look,
That awes with strange repulsion. There, the bird
Sings never merrily in the sombre trees,
That seem to have never known a term of youth,
Their young leaves all being blighted. A rank growth
Spreads venomously round, with power to taint;
And blistering dews await the thoughtless hand
That rudely parts the thicket. Cypresses,
Each a great ghastly giant, old and gray,
Stride o'er the dusk, dank tract,—with buttresses
Spread round, apart, not seeming to sustain,
Yet link'd by secret twines, that, underneath,
Blend with each arching trunk. Fantastic vines,
That swing like monstrous serpents in the sun,
Bind top to top, until the encircling trees
Group all in close embrace. Vast skeletons

Of forests, that have perish'd ages gone,
Molder, in mighty masses, on the plain;
Now buried in some dark and mystic tarn,
Or sprawl'd above it, resting on great arms,
And making, for the opossum and the fox,
Bridges, that help them as they roam by night.
Alternate stream and lake, between the banks,
Glimmer in doubtful light: smooth, silent, dark,
They tell not what they harbor; but, beware!

Lest, rising to the tree on which you stand,
You sudden see the moccasin snake heave up
His yellow shining belly and flat head
Of burnish'd copper. Stretch'd at length, behold
Where yonder Cayman, in his natural home,
The mammoth lizard, all his armor on,
Slumbers half-buried in the sedgy grass,
Beside the green ooze where he shelters him.
The place, so like the gloomiest realm of death,
Is yet the abode of thousand forms of life,
The terrible, the beautiful, the strange,—winged
And creeping creatures, such as make the
Instinctive flesh with apprehension crawl,

When sudden we behold. Hark! at our voice
The whooping crane, gaunt fisher in these realms,
Erects his skeleton form and shrieks in flight,
On great white wings. A pair of summer ducks,
Most princely in their plumage, as they hear
His cry, with senses quickening all to fear,
Dash up from the lagoon with marvellous haste,
Following his guidance. See! aroused by these,
And startled by our progress o'er the stream,
The steel-jaw'd Cayman, from his grassy slope,
Slides silent to the slimy green abode,
Which is his province.

You behold him now,
His bristling back uprising as he speeds
To safety, in the centre of the lake,
Whence his head peers alone,—a shapeless knot,
That shows no sign of life; the hooded eye,
Nathless, being ever vigilant and sharp,
Measuring the victim. See! a butterfly,
That, travelling all the day, has counted climes
Only by flowers, to rest himself a while,

And, as a wanderer in a foreign land,
To pause and look around him ere he goes,
Lights on the monster's brow. The surly mute
Straightway goes down; so suddenly, that he,
The dandy of the summer flowers and woods,
Dips his light wings, and soils his golden coat,
With the rank waters of the turbid lake.
Wondering and vex'd, the pluméd citizen
Flies with an eager terror to the banks,
Seeking more genial natures,—but in vain.
Here are no gardens such as he desires,
No innocent flowers of beauty, no delights
Of sweetness free from taint. The genial growth
He loves, finds here no harbor. Fetid shrubs,
That scent the gloomy atmosphere, offend
His pure patrician fancies.

On the trees,
That look like felon spectres, he beholds
No blossoming beauties; and for smiling heavens,
That flutter his wings with breezes of pure balm,
He nothing sees but sadness—aspects dread,
That gather frowning, cloud and fiend in one,
As if in combat, fiercely to defend
Their empire from the intrusive wing and beam.
The example of the butterfly be ours.
He spreads his lacquer'd wings above the trees,
And speeds with free flight, warning us to seek
For a more genial home, and couch more sweet
Than these drear borders offer us to-night.

# Present State of LettersExcerpt from an extensively lengthy letter to William Gilmore Simms. Published in the Southern Literary Messenger (July 1844, pp., 410,411)

*T. William Gilmore Simms, Esq.*

DEAR SIR,

It is a little more than a year since I had the pleasure of a prolonged and interesting conversation with you, in Charleston, on the subject of American Literature. This conversation may have passed from your memory, for to you it was merely the easy enunciation of thoughts long entertained, and, doubtless frequently expressed before. I shall not as readily forget it, for it has been to me the germ of much subsequent reflection on the nature of the Literature in general, and more especially of the Literature of this country.

The seed you cast lightly on the soil has sprouted, put forth leaves and fructified, and, though the fruit so produced may be crude, still it may be suggestive of profounder and more mature views to others, able to devote more time and ability to the investigation of the subject than I can. In resolving to give publicity to my meditations, I have preferred the epistolary form to that of the more imposing essay, as I design expressing my views in that loose and desultory manner in which they rise, and which is perhaps the most suitable for the utterance of opinions for whose soundness I will not vouch, and which futire reflection may possibly induce me to modify, or even abandon.

And I do not think that I can address my remarks to any one with greater propriety than to yourself, for you were the original cause of their formulation-you have devoted much care to the examination of the subject-and you have been lately illustrating kindred topics with signal ability. Moreover, I know that you will overlook any crudity which may be incident to this inartistic expression of my opinions, and to the undisguised nature of the speculations themselves. I shall, therefore, presume your indulgent consideration, even in those instances in which you may be disposed to dissent altogether from my conclusions; and having anticipated your favor. I shall be less apprehensive of a failure to obtain that of others.

But the latest instance is the most instructive of all; the rise of the Byronic and the Lake Schools of Poetry in England, and the appearance of the modern French Literature as soon as the fanaticism of social change had subsided into a less violent ferment in France, show how suddenly and how profoundly political convictions operate upon the literary world. Byron and his imitators were the highest and last expression of a system which was passing away; but mingled with this, and in much bolder prominence, was the utterance of those feelings of dark uncertainty, of skepticism and of despair, produced in apprehensive minds by the whirl and confusion of tottering creeds and crumbling institutions which filled the world at the time when they wrote.

These three, Byron, Wordsworth and Shelley, were equally in harmony with their own times, and with the social phenomena succeeding the outburst of the French Revolution, but they regarded the world around them from different points of view and hence arose the stronger features of their dissimilarity.Byron was, however, the truest as well as the most rhythmical exponent of his age. He uttered the common but indistinct feelings of men of that day in the most beautiful and poetic form-the melancholy occasioned by the departure of a former system-the full intelligence of the discord and ruin around-and a sad despair of any better fruits, but only the fear of deeper and deeper degradation:- these were the feelings which gave inspiration to Byron, but to them was added new poignancy from the unhappy events of his life, which never suffered him to be in harmony himself with the external world around him. To use his own words, his experience made him feel that –

*Our life is a false nature, it is not in*
*the harmony of things.*

We are still in the gloom of twilight, but we know that the day will soon break, so that our uncertainty manifests itself under less exaggerated forms; but it exists not the less on this account. As far as the poetry of doubt is concerned-that is irrevocably gone-Byron's harp is unstrung; the fountain once so prolific of melody is no more-the dead bones cannot be revived by the wand of the enchanter-that phase of society of which he was the utterance can never return-the sources of his poetry are exhausted, and his poetry belongs to the past.

The same may be said, though in a different degree of Wordsworth and Shelley. The circumstances-the age which produced them have departed, and though they are rather the prophets of the future than the reproducers of the past, yet when another birth of poetry shall be vouchsafed to us, it will have its own peculiar characteristics, as it will be due to its own peculiar causes.

***Very sincerely and respectfully,***
***Your obliged and obedient servant,***
***George Frederick Holmes,***
***Orangeburg, S.C.***

Published in the ***Southern Literary Messenger***
**July 1844, pp., 410,411 –part)**

# MARY E. HEWITT

Mary Hewitt was born in 1807 and died in 1894. When Mary was three, her father died. Her mother moved with her from Malden, to Boston, Massachusetts. She grew up in Boston and later married James L. Hewitt on New York. Later, James Hewitt passed away and she married R. Stebbins in 1854.

Mary wrote several poems, they were published in periodicals such as 'Southern Literary Messenger', who printed her poem 'A Bivouac in the Desert' in their issue July 1844.

In 1845 she published 'Songs of our Land' in 1850 she edited the book, 'Gem of the Western World' and in 1851 edited a memorial to Frances S. Osgood. In 1864 she published 'Poems, Sacred, Passionate and Legendary'.

During the 1840's Edgar Allan Poe was an Editor for the 'Southern Literary Messenger' on a couple of occasions he mentioned the following of her works.

"Her compositions evince poetic fervor, classicism and keen appreciation of both moral and physical beauty. No one of them, perhaps can be judiciously commended as a whole, but no one of them is without merit."

In 1846, Edgar Allan Poe described her in his "The Literati of New York City. No. VI," in ***Godey's Lady's Book***, v. 33, p. 159:

> In character she is sincere, fervent, benevolent, with a heart full of the truest charity— sensitive to praise and to blame; in temperament, melancholy (although this is not precisely the term); in manner, subdued, gentle, yet with grace and dignity; converses impressively, earnestly, yet quietly and in a low tone. In person she is tall and slender, with black hair and large gray eyes; complexion also dark; the general expression of the countenance singularly interesting and agreeable.

## *A Bivouac in the Desert*

## Introduction to the poem

"After the battle of the Pyramids, the whole way through the desert was tracked with the bones and bodies of men and animals, who had perished in these dreadful wastes. In order to warm themselves at night, they gathered together the dry bones and bodies of the dead, which the vultures had spared and ***it was by a fire composed of this fuel that Napoleon lay down to sleep in the desert!"***
***—Miot's Memoirs***

***A Bivouac in the Desert***

The ploughshare of the conqueror passed
Across the burning desert plain;
While on the sower followed fast,
And scattered in the bright red grain.

And tracking on that welded blade,
Forged from their countless battle-brands;
Far o'er the broad, deep furrow made,
On swept his trained Praetorian bands.

The vulture is the desert's king!
And what of conqueror's recketh he?
Who bounds his empire by his wing,
Reigneth, I ween, right fearlessly!

'Twas night-the conqueror's harvest night-
No star in heaven its glories hid;
And poured the moon her radiant light,
On desert, tent, and pyramid.

The reaper's blade its toil forsook-
And in the glittering river Nile,
The plumed and turban'd Mameluke,
Slept with the scale-armed crocodile.

Oh, Isis ! Thou adored of old,
With mystic rite, and symbol rare;
Rude hands have rent thy veil's dark fold,
And lain thy hidden altars bare.

The crescent gleams from Moslem tower,
High o'er the walls of Ptolemy;
And naught but thine own lotos flower,
Oh, Nilus ! bends to worship thee.

Where 'mid the tombs their grandeur raised,
Her Pharoahs slumber, all forgot;
Remnant of Egypt's pride abased,
The Copht her power remembers not-

Ages of sceptred glory gone,
Your sculptured records time hath kept,
Where'er to conquest thindering on,
To victory, aye Sesostris swept.[1]

Egypt ! Nile's suckling ! Thou that wast,
Throned in the old world's infancy-
While yet on her kind, fostering breast,
The teeming earth encradled thee-

How, through all time, a doomed lot
Hath been thine own-devoted land !
For aye the scourge that wearieth not-
For aye, for aye the foeman's brand !

Sleep they, the hosts thy sands that trod?
Lo ! with their centuries, vanquished all
Yet, where the conquering Persian stood,
Where warred the Assyrian, wars the Gaul

---

[1] "We are assured on the personal evidence of Herodotus and Strabo, that the pillars erected by the Egyptian leader to mark his conquests, still remained in their days, and that they were even personally inspected by them in Syria, Palestine, Arabia and Ethiopia. The inscription which these proud monuments every where bore, was to the following effect; "Sespstris, King of Kings, and Lord of Lords, subdued this country by his arms." – ***Civil History of Ancient Egypt.***

The jackal and the wolf are out,
A phantom army holds the plain;
Why pales the conqueror? Is't with fear
His blood runs chill through every vein?

Fear ! Was't a word for him who played
The sword 'gainst crown and sceptre old?
Write FEAR where drave his furrowing blade
Who trembled but beneath the cold !

Ho ! Ye that reaped the ripened field-
What left ye to the gleaner's hand ?
Her stubble let the desert yield,
To cheer this wide, unvarying sand !

For leagues away, the barren plain
Nor tree, nor shrub, nor verdure owns-
Where they had sown, the blood-red grain,
They gleaned but blanched, and mouldering bones.

And where of old the cloud and fire
Led on the wandering Israelite,
They heaped the pile-till far the pyre
Reared its red column on the night.

And fast the fanning night-wind came,
And high the scroll accusing swept;
While 'neath that uplift tongue of flame,
The "Lion of the Desert" SLEPT![2]

[2] "Napoleon," says Sir Walter Scott, "was pleased with the flattery which derived his christian name from the Greek words, signifying the "Lion of the Desert".

# THE HUTCHINSON FAMILY

John Hutchinson and three of his brothers (Asa, Jesse, and Judson) named themselves the' Hutchinson Family Singers'. They gave their first concert in Milford, New Hampshire, in 1840 and performed in Lynn the following year. They were the children of Jesse and Mary Hutchinson. The Hutchison Family singers were often referred to as, "The Tribe of Jesse".

The group took up various causes. Some of these were abolitionism, temperance, and women's rights. In December 1842, John Hutchinson signed a petition affiliated with an abolitionist rally in Milford. By the following year, the Hutchinsons had become ***vocal abolitionists***.

In 1843 an antislavery convention was held in Milford attended by Wm. Lloyd Garrison.From this point on decided to exert their influence and composed and sang antislavery songs.
At certain concerts some of the audience became unruly. On several occasions when they sang, mobs tried to break up the meetings. The group often faced unfriendly behavior. Frank Carpenter, the artist and writer, knew Abby well. He said that, when she and her brothers sang their songs of freedom, Abby, "would look directly into the eyes of the mob leaders, invariably with the effect of subduing the unruly spirits."

The Hutchinsons' performed across New England in 1842, taking in as much as $130 per performance. In 1843, Jesse wrote "The Old Granite State", a song about the Hutchinson family, their origins in New Hampshire, and their itinerant lifestyle. The song became their signature number.

American newspapers of the time were trumpeting "native talent", and critics responded favorably to the Hutchinsons' early concerts, although they did express misgivings about the group's song selection.

After their first New York City concert on May 13, 1843, the ***New York Tribune*** wrote:

> They gave a concert on Saturday evening and acquitted themselves quite well. They know how to make music, decidedly, though some of their songs are not well chosen either to gratify the audience or exhibit their peculiar powers. We wish they would take care to favor the unscientific public with the words of their songs distinctly. Russell does so, and it is to thousands one of the best points of his singing.

When the Hutchinsons' advertised in the ***Herald*** on May 13, 1843 that their program featured "their most popular Quartettes, Trios, Solos, such as have not failed to please fashionable audiences in Boston and many other cities and towns in New England."

After the death of Elizabeth, her sister, Abby joined Asa, John and Jesse on a successful tour of Europe in 1845. They traveled with Frederick Douglass in England in 1845 and stayed for almost a year. They sang original songs such as, "Get Off the Track!", "Right over Wrong", and "The Slave's Appeal".

They toured Great Britain. Meanwhile, Caleb, Joshua, Rhoda, and Zephaniah Hutchinson toured the United States under the name Home Branch of the Hutchinson Family. When the original group returned, they angrily put an end to the Home Branch. The Hutchinsons added several original songs at this time. In 1850, Abby Hutchinson wrote "Song of Our Mountain Home", It included the line, "Among our free hills are true hearts and brave, / The air of our mountains ne'er breathed on a slave."

## Other 'Singing' Familes contemporary with the Hutchinson Family

Contemporary with the Hutchinson Family were the Bakers also from New Hampshire with their own song repertoire 'arranged by John C.Baker). The Bakers were popular with their renditions of, "The Happiest Time is Now", "The Mountaineer's Farewell" in 1847. John C.Baker's individual 'Hit' was "The Burman Lover", or "The Little Canoe.

There was also a Barker Family who sang, "The Graves of a Household" in 1848 and a Blakely Family with their, "Softly, Lightly, Sweetly Sing and the Gibson Family with their rendition of "We Are Wandering o'er the Mountain in 1853.

**Get Off The Track!**
***Jesse Hutchinson, Jr.***

Ho! the car, Emancipation,
Rides majestic thro' our nation
Bearing on its train, the story
Liberty! a nation's glory.

Roll it along! Roll it along!
Roll it along! thro' the nation
Freedom's car, Emancipation

Roll it along! Roll it along!
Roll it along! thro' the nation
Freedom's car, Emancipation.
Men of various predilections,
Frightened, run in all directions;
Merchants, editors, physicians,
Lawyers, priests and politicians.

Get out of the way! Get out of the way!
Get out of the way! every station,
Clear the track of 'mancipation.

Get out of the way! Get out of the way!
Get out of the way! every station,
Clear the track of 'mancipation.

All true friends of emancipation,
Haste to freedom's rail road station;
Quick into the cars get seated,
All is ready, and completed.

Put on the steam! Put on the steam!
Put on the steam! All are crying,
And the liberty flags are flying.
Put on the steam! Put on the steam!
Put on the steam! All are crying,
And the liberty flags are flying.
Hear the mighty car wheels humming!
Now look out! the engine's coming!
Church and statesmen! hear the thunder!
Clear the track! or you'll fall under.

Get off the track! Get off the track!
Get off the track! all are singing,
While the liberty bell is ringing.
Get off the track! Get off the track!
Get off the track! all are singing,
While the liberty bell is ringing.
See the people run to meet us;
At the depots thousands greet us;
All take seats with exultation,
In the car, Emancipation.

Huzza! Huzza! Huzza! Huzza!
Huzza! Huzza! Emancipation
Soon will bless our happy nation.

Huzza! Huzza! Huzza! Huzza!
Huzza! Huzza! Emancipation
Soon will bless our happy nation.
Huzza!

**The Old Granite State**
*by Jesse Hutchinson, Jr.*

We have come from the mountains, we have come from the mountains
We have come from the mountains of the Old Granite State.
We're a band of brothers, we're a band of brothers
We're a band of brothers and we live among the hills
With a band of music, with a band of music
With a band of music we are passing 'round the world.

We have left our aged parents, we have left our aged parents
We have left our aged parents in the Old Granite State.
We obtained their blessing, we obtained their blessing
We obtained their blessing and we bless them in return.
Good old fashioned singers, good old fashioned singers
Good old fashioned singers they can make the air resound.

Yes while the air is ringing with their wild mountain singing
We the news to you are bringing from the Old Granite State.
'Tis the Tribe of Jesse, 'Tis the Tribe of Jesse
'Tis the Tribe of Jesse and their several names we sing.

David, Noah, Andrew, Zephy, Caleb, Joshua, Jess, and Benjy,
Judson, Rhoda, John and Asa, and Abby are our names.
We're the Sons of Mary of the Tribe of Jesse
And we now address ye with our native mountain song.

Liberty is our motto, liberty is our motto
Equal liberty is our motto in the Old Granite State.
We despise oppression, we despise oppression
We despise oppression and we cannot be enslaved.

Yes we're friends of emancipation and we'll sing the proclamation
'Til it echoes through our nation from the Old Granite State
That the Tribe of Jesse, that the Tribe of Jesse
That the Tribe of Jesse are the friends of equal rights.

Like our sires before us, we will swell the chorus
Till the heavens aura shall resound the loud huzzah
Hurrah, hurrah, hurrah
Hurrah, hurrah, hurrah

# David Crockett (also known as Davy Crockett)

His personal motto - ***"Be always sure you're right-then go a-head!"***

David "Davy" Crockett, was born in Greene County, Tennessee, August 17.1786. He died at the battle of the Alamo in 1836. In his youth he worked as a Wagoner also as a laborer. In 1806 he married Mary 'Polly' Finlay of Jefferson County. From 1811 after having two sons they moved to live in the mountains of East Tennessee. Later he enlisted in the militia as a scout in the Creek Indian War campaign in November 1813

He was under the command of the celebrated future President, Andrew Jackson. After his enlistment in the Creek Indian War expired he returned home. When the 'Battle of New Orleans occurred he re-enlisted September 28th 1814 as a sergeant. He arrived on November 7th the day after Jackson took Pensacola, and spent his time trying to ferret out the British-trained Indians from the Florida swamps. After his discharge in 1815 he returned home. His wife Polly died the following year.

On May 21, 1815, Crockett was elected a lieutenant in the Thirty-second Militia regiment of Franklin County. He married Elizabeth Patton, a widow with two children. The following year the family moved to Lawrence County, Tennessee and settled at the head of Shoal Creek. He then continued his political and military career. After a brief stint at being a Justice of the Peace, he then became the town commissioner of Lawrenceburg, and was elected colonel of the Fifty-seventh Militia regiment in the county that same year. (1818)

New Year's Day 1821 marked a turning point in Crockett's career. He ran as commissioner for a seat in the Tennessee legislature as the representative of Lawrence and Hickman counties. He won the August election and, from the beginning, took an active interest in public land policy regarding the West. After the session concluded he moved his family to Gibson County in West Tennessee and was reelected in 1823, He was defeated in August 1825 in his first bid for a seat in Congress. In 1826 after returning to private business, Crockett nearly died when his boats carrying barrel staves were wrecked in the Mississippi River.

He was brought to Memphis and encouraged to run again for Congress by Maj. M. B. Winchester and won election over Gen. William Arnold and Col. Adam Alexander to the United States House of Representatives in 1827. He was re-elected to a second term in 1829 and differed with President Andrew Jackson and the Tennessee delegation on several issues, including land reform and the Indian removal bill. In his 1831 campaign for a third term, Crockett openly and vehemently attacked Jackson's policies and was defeated in a close election by William Fitzgerald.

Crockett's reputation as a sharpshooter, hunter, and yarn-spinner had attracted national attention. ***Life and Adventures of Colonel David Crockett of West Tennessee*** was published in 1833 and reprinted the same year under the more accurate title of ***Sketches and Eccentricities of Colonel David Crockett of West Tennessee.***

His extraneous life was described in popular books during the period 1835 to 1856 often published under his own name. They were responsible for creating the legend of ‘Davy Crockett’. He was discontent due to ***the inaccuracy of events attributed to him***, he made reference to these false character portrayals in his own autobiography.

In 1833 he returned to Congress. In 1834, he published his autobiography (assisted by Thomas Chilton), ***A Narrative of the Life of David Crockett of the State of Tennessee, the only book that David ever wrote***. In 1835 he lost his congressional campaign to a lawyer supported by Jackson and by Governor Carroll of Tennessee by a small margin of votes. He became discontented with political life and decided to move west with his family to Texas on November 1, 1835, departed and noted that he was planning, "to explore the Texas well before I return."

He had no plans in mind to join the popular fight to establish Texas independence (at that time, it was Spanish territory). At a farewell gathering in Memphis with friends he made his famous comment, "Since you have chosen to elect a man with a timber toe to succeed me, you may all go to hell and I will go to Texas." With several others he left the next day on a route down the Mississippi River to the Arkansas, from there up-river to Little Rock, then overland to Fulton, Arkansas, up the Red River along the northern boundary of Texas; across the Red River, through Clarksville, to Nacogdoches and San Augustine; and on to San Antonio.

At San Augustine the party evidently divided. ***Crockett and Patton signed the oath of allegiance,*** but only after Crockett insisted upon the insertion of the word "republican" in the document. They then swore their allegiance to the "Provisional Government of Texas or any future ***republican*** Government that would be declared." His enthusiasm over Texas is evident in a letter he wrote, January 9, 1836,

> "I must say as to what I have seen of Texas it is the garden spot of the world. The best land and the best prospects for health I ever saw, and I do believe it is a fortune to any man to come here. There is a world of country here to settle. . .
>
> I have taken the oath of government and have enrolled my name as a volunteer and will set out for the Rio Grand in a few days with the volunteers from the United States. But all volunteers is entitled to vote for a member of the convention or to be voted for, and I have but little doubt of being elected a member to form a constitution for this province. I am rejoiced at my fate. I had rather be in my present situation than to be elected to a seat in Congress for life. I am in hopes of making a fortune yet for myself and family, bad as my prospect has been."

He intended to become land agent for the new territory.

# The Alamo - Crockett's Diary

Crocket kept a diary[1] and his notes whilst he was in San Antonio showed him in high spirits, although he indicated that he had a shortage of provisions. On February 23rd. the enemy were in sight and the little garrison resolved to defend the Alamo. They made a large flag with thirteen stripes, red and white alternately on a blue background, with a large white star in the center, and between the points, the word "Texas. Over the next nine days he wrote an account of their sufferings and their brave defense.

On March 3rd, he indicated that they had given up all hope of receiving any assistance from outside so they promised to fight on to the end and in dying to kill as many of the enemy combatants.

***His diary entry for March 4th, stated;***

> Shells have been falling into the fort like hail during the day, but without effect. About dusk this evening we saw a man running toward the fort pursued by about a dozen Mexican cavalry
>
> The bee hunter[2] immediately recognized him as the old pirate who had gone to Goliad for assistance, and calling to two others, the bee hunter sallied out of the fort to the relief of the old man, I followed close after. Before we reached him the Mexicans were close upon his heels. He stopped suddenly, turned short upon his pursuers, discharge his rifle, and saw one of his enemies fall from his horse. After running a short distance again, the old pirate, finding that he would be taken and cut to pieces, turned fiercely, and to the amazement of the enemy clubbed his gun and dashed among them like a wounded tiger.
>
> By the time we reached him, his pursuers had fled like sparrows and in the ardor of the moment we followed them some distance, not seeing that our retreat was cut off by another detachment of cavalry. Nothing was to be done but to fight our way through. They were about twenty in number and stood their ground while we dashed among them, and for about five minutes a bloody conflict ensued. Then a detachment was seen coming from the fort to our relief, and the Mexicans scampered away, leaving eight of their men dead upon the field.

[1] Refer to the diary found in 1975 which is an accurate account of the death of Crockett and his fellow defenders, as recorded by a contemporary Mexican combatant.

[2] Earlier they had mentioned another in their group of defenders was a bee hunter from Nacogdoches, Texas also another person, a fierce old man, had been a pirate but had abandoned the sea.

We did not escape unscathed, for both the pirate and the bee hunter were mortally wounded, and I received a saber cut across the forehead.

The old man died without speaking as soon as we entered the fort. We bore my young friend to his bed, dressed his wounds, and I watched beside him. He lay without complaint or manifesting pain, until about midnight, when he spoke. I asked him what he wanted. "Nothing," he replied with a sigh that seemed to rend his heart, and his eyes filled with tears as he continued his 'Poor Kate of Nacogdoches; her words were prophetic, Colonel.' Then he sang in a low voice,- 'But toom' cam' the saddle, all bluidy to see, and hane cam' the steed, but hame never cam' he, "He spoke no more, an a few minutes afterward died.

Poor Kate, who will tell this to thee?

The last entry in Crockett's diary bears the date March 5$^{th}$. It is as follows: "Pop, pop, pop! Bom, bom, bom! throughout the day.- No time for memorandums now,- Go ahead!-Liberty and independence forever!"

## The true account of his death

From a contemporary enemy combatant's diary, discovered in 1975.

In early February Crockett arrived at San Antonio de Béxar; Antonio López de Santa Anna arrived on February 20. He joined up with Col. William B. Travis, who had disregarded Sam Houston's orders to withdraw from the Alamo, rather than support Houston, a Jackson sympathizer. He saw his future path in the struggle to establish an independent Texas.

Crockett died in battle of the Alamo on March 6, 1836. The manner of his death was uncertain, however, until the publication in 1975 of the diary of Lt. José Enrique de la Peña. Susanna Dickinson, wife of Almaron Dickinson, an officer at the Alamo, said Crockett died on the outside, one of the earliest to fall. Joe, Travis's slave and the only male Texan to survive the battle, reported seeing Crockett lying dead with slain Mexicans around him and stated that only one man, named Warner, surrendered to the Mexicans (Warner was taken to Santa Anna and promptly shot)

When Peña's eyewitness account was placed together with other corroborating documents, Crockett's central part in the defense became clear. Travis had previously written that during the first bombardment Crockett was everywhere in the Alamo "animating the men to do their duty."

Other reports told of the deadly fire of his rifle that killed five Mexican gunners in succession, as they each attempted to fire a cannon bearing on the fort, and that he may have just missed Santa Anna, who thought himself out of range of all the defenders' rifles. Crockett and five or six others were captured when the Mexican troops took the Alamo at about six o'clock that morning, even though Santa Anna had ordered that no prisoners be taken.

The general, infuriated when some of his officers brought the Americans before him to try to intercede for their lives, ordered them executed immediately. They were bayoneted and then shot. Crockett's reputation and that of the other survivors was not, as some have suggested, sullied by their capture. Their dignity and bravery was, in fact, further underscored by Peña's recounting that "these unfortunates died without complaining and without humiliating themselves before their torturers."

Daniel Boone was the rough-hewn representative of frontier independence and virtue. In this regard, the motto he adopted and made famous epitomized his spirit: ***"Be always sure you're right-then go a-head!"***

## Bibliography

Michael A. Lofaro, "Crockett, David," ***Handbook of Texas Online*****,** s.v." http://www.tshaonline.org/handbook/online/articles/CC/fcr24.html (accessed April 29, 2010), by kind permission of “Handbook of Texas Online.”

# LYDIA SIGOURNEY

Lydia Sigourney; (Maiden name; Lydia Howard Huntley)

## September 1, 1791 – June 10, 1865

Lydia was a popular American poet during the early and mid 19th century. She was known as the "Sweet Singer of Hartford". Most of her works were published under her married name.She was born in Norwich, Connecticut to Ezekiel Huntley and Zerviah Wentworth. and was their only child , she was named after her father's first wife, Lydia Howard, who had died soon after marrying Ezekiel.

She was educated in Norwich and Hartford. After conducting a private school for young ladies in Norwich, she conducted a similar school in Hartford from 1814 until 1819.

She described her relation to her parents, in her autobiography of her decision to care for them, and her intent to avoid marriage because it would interfere with this relationship.

> I had ***reason for avoiding serious advances***. My mind was made up never to leave my parents.

> I felt that their absorbing love could never be repaid by the longest life-service, and that the responsibility of an only child, their sole prop and solace, would be strictly regarded by Him who readeth the heart. I had seen aged people surrounded by indifferent persons, who considered their care a burden, and could not endure the thought that my tender parents, who were without near relatives, should be thrown upon the fluctuating kindness of hirelings and strangers. To me, my father already seemed aged, though scarcely sixty; and I said, in my musing hours, Shall he, who never denied me aught, or spoke to me otherwise than in love-tones, stretch forth his hands in their weakness, "and find none to gird him"?

On June 16, 1819, she married Charles Sigourney, and after her marriage chose to write anonymously in "leisure" time. It was not until her parents were in dire need and her husband had lost some of his former affluence that she began to write as an occupation. When she was referred to as the probable author of the anonymous ***Letters to Young Ladies, By a Lady*** she admitted authorship and began to write openly as Mrs. Sigourney.

After her death, John Greenleaf Whittier composed a poem for her memorial tablet:

***She sang alone, ere womanhood had known***
***The gift of song which fills the air to-day:***
***Tender and sweet, a music all her own***
***May fitly linger where she knelt to pray.***

This passage outlined her main themes of old age, death, responsibility, religion, and of her a strong belief in God and the Christian faith - and work . She often wrote elegies or poems for recently deceased neighbors, friends, and acquaintances. Her work is one example of Victorian-era death literature which views death as ***an escape to a better place, especially for children.***

A contemporary critic called her work, infused with morals, "more like the dew than the lightning". She enjoyed substantial popularity in her lifetime and earned several nicknames, including "the American Hemans", the "Sweet Singer of Hartford", and the "female Milton".

Her influences included the work of Hannah More, William Wordsworth, and William Cowper.

Over the years, her writings have been overlooked or forgotten. When remembered, she has been criticized unfairly[1] for being too shallow or for catering to the society in which she lived where women were expected to avoid public lives. However, recently there has been a renewed interest in Sigourney, particularly among feminist literary scholars.

She was one of the most popular writers of her day, both in America and in England, and was called 'the American Hemans.' Her writings were characterized by fluency, grace and quiet reflection on nature, domestic and religious life, and often too sentimental. Some of her blank verse and pictures of nature suggest Bryant. Among her most successful poems are 'Niagara' and 'Indian Names.'

Rev. E. B. Huntington wrote a small consideration of Mrs. Sigourney's life shortly after her death. He thought that her success came "because with [her] gifts and [her] success, she had with singular kindliness of heart made her very life-work itself a constant source of blessing and joy to others. Her very goodness had made her great. Her genial goodwill had given her power. Her loving friendliness had made herself and her name everywhere a charm." She wrote to inspire others and Huntingdon felt that she had been successful.

In 1844, Sigourney, Iowa, the county seat of Keokuk County, Iowa, was named in her honor. A large oil-painted portrait of Lydia still graces the foyer of the county courthouse.

## Lyceum Movement

Sigourney's commitment to education, writing, and charity was testimony to women's possibilities for self-betterment and, no doubt, a role model for women. When Sigourney gave up her anonymity for good, she became the most widely known "authoress" and "poetess" in America. As a result, during the lyceum movement that flourished in the United States in the 19th century, women named literary societies and study clubs in her honor.

---

[1] It was rather caustic to crticize her so. She was writing in a normal style, with some piety not uncharacterstic with her contemporary audience, and cognizant of the strictness of behaviour and expressed herself in the best mannerthat a woman of that period could do. (R.D. Morritt).

The Lyceum Movement reached the peak of its popularity in the antebellum era. Public Lyceums were set up around the country, as far as Florida and Detroit. Transcendentalists such as Ralph Waldo Emerson and Henry David Thoreau endorsed the movement and gave speeches at many local lyceums. As a young man, Abraham Lincoln gave a speech to a Lyceum in Springfield, Illinois.

The lyceums, mechanics' institutes, and agriculture organizations that flourished in the United States before and after the Civil War were important in the development of adult education in America. During this period hundreds of informal associations were established for the purpose of improving the social, intellectual, and moral fabric of society.

## Poems

***LIFE***

LIFE is like a painted dream,
Like the rapid summer stream,
Like the flashing meteor's ray,
Like the shortest winter's day,
Like the fitful breeze that sighs,
Like the wavering flame that dies,
Darting dazzling on the eye,
Fading in eternity.

***VAIN PURSUITS***

Some rejoice in pleasure's beam,
Some in fortune's glittering stream,
Some in beauty, some in pride,
Some in honour's treacherous tide;
While with giddy haste they pass
Like the insect o'er the grass.

***INDIAN SUMMER***

WHEN was the redman's summer?
When the rose
Hung its first banner out? When the gray rock,
Or the brown heath, the radiant kalmia clothed?
Or when the loiterer by the reedy brooks
Started to see the proud lobelia glow
Like living flame? When through the forest gleamed
The rhododendron? Or the fragrant breath
Of the magnolia swept deliciously
Over the half-laden nerve?

When the groves
In fleeting colours wrote their own decay,
And leaves fell eddying on the sharpen'd blast
That sang their dirge; when o'er their rustling bed
The red deer sprang, or fled the shrill-voiced quail,
Heavy of wing and fearful; when, with heart
Foreboding or depress'd, the white man mark'd
The signs of coming winter: then began
The Indian's joyous season. Then the haze,
Soft and illusive as a fairy dream,
Lapp'd all the landscape in its silvery fold.
The quiet rivers, that were wont to hide
'Neath shelving banks, beheld their course betray'd
By the white mist that o'er their foreheads crept,
While wrapp'd in morning dreams, the sea and sky
Slept 'neath one curtain, as if both were merged
In the same element. Slowly the sun,
And all reluctantly, the spell dissolved,
And then it took upon its parting wing
A rainbow glory.

Gorgeous was the time
Yet brief as gorgeous. Beautiful to thee,
Our brother hunter, but to us replete
With musing thoughts in melancholy train.
Our joys, alas! too oft were woe to thee.
Yet ah! poor Indian! whom we fain would drive
Both from our hearts, and from thy father's lands,
The perfect year doth bear thee on its crown,
And when we would forget, repeat thy name.

### *THE SUSCEPTIBLE MIND*

HAST thou seen the Mimosa within its soft cell,
All shrinking and suffering stand,
And draw in its tendrils, and fold its young leaves,
From the touch of the tenderest hand ?
Hast thou seen the young Aspen that trembles
and sighs,
On the breath of the lingering wind ?
Oh ! Ihese are but emblems, imperfect and faint
Of the shrinking and sensitive mind.

### *THE QUEEN OF NIGHT*

THE queen of night rode hold and high,
Her path was white with stars,
Her cheek was sanguine, and her eye
Glanc'd on the blood stain'd Mars.

No word she spake, no sign .she made,
Save that her head she bow'd,
As if a cold, good night she bade.
To some departing cloud.

A fleecy robe was loosely cast,
Around her graceful form,
She hid her forehead from the blast,
Hoarse herald of the storm.

But soon she staid her rushing car,
And check'd her rapid rein,
For morn beheld her from afar,
And frown'd upon her train.

The queen of night, and rosy morn,
Together might not dwell;
One came to rouse the slumbering dawn
The other sought her cell.

### *RAPIDITY OF TIME.*

EV'N while we pause, the rapid date
Of life comes rushing on,
The sad heart feels the stroke of fate,
We tremble and are gone:

Gone and forgot, the mourning eye
May moisten as we sleep;
But time shall sooth the rushing sigh,
And dry the eyes that weep.

A little mound of turf, alone
Shall shade our senseless breast;
The clay-cold sod, the burial stone,
Made dark with storms, with moss overgrown.
Shall mark our place of rest.

### *THE CORAL INSECT*

Toil on! toil on! ye ephemeral train,
Who build in the tossing and treacherous main ;
Toil on,—for the wisdom of man ye mock,
With your sand-based structures and domes of rock;
Your columns the fathomless fountains lave,
And your arches spring up to the crested wave;
Ye're a puny race, this to boldly rear
A fabric so vast, in a realm so drear.
Ye bind the deep with your secret zone,
The ocean is seal'd, and the surge a stone;
Fresh wreaths from the coral pavement spring,
Like the terraced pride of Assyria's king;
The turf looks green where the breakers roll'd;
O'er the whirlpool ripens the rind of gold;
The sea-snatch'd isle is the home of men,
And mountains exult where the wave hath been.
But why do you plant 'neath the billows dark
The wrecking reef for the gallant bark?
There are snares enough on the tented field,

'Mid the blossom'd sweets that the valleys yield;
There are serpents to coil, ere the flowers are up;
There's a poison-drop in man's purest cup,
There are foes that watch for his cradle breath,
And why need ye sow the floods with death?

With mouldering bones the deeps are white,
From the ice-clad pole to the tropics bright;—
The mermaid hath twisted her fingers cold
With the mewsh of the sea-boy's curls of gold,
And the gods of ocean have frown'd to see
The mariner's bed in their halls of glee;—
Hath earth no graves, that ye thus must spread
The boundless sea for the thronging dead?
Ye build,--ye build,--but ye enter not in,
Like the tribes whom the desert devour'd in their sin;
From the land of promise ye fade and die,
Ere its verdure gleams forth on your weary eye;—
As athe kings of the cloud-crown'd pyramid,
Their noteless bonds in oblivion hid;
Ye slumber unmark'd 'mid the desolate main,
While the wonder and pride of your works remain.

Copy of a letter written by Lydia Sigourney to Mrs. Sarah P. Baldwin upon the death of her mother:

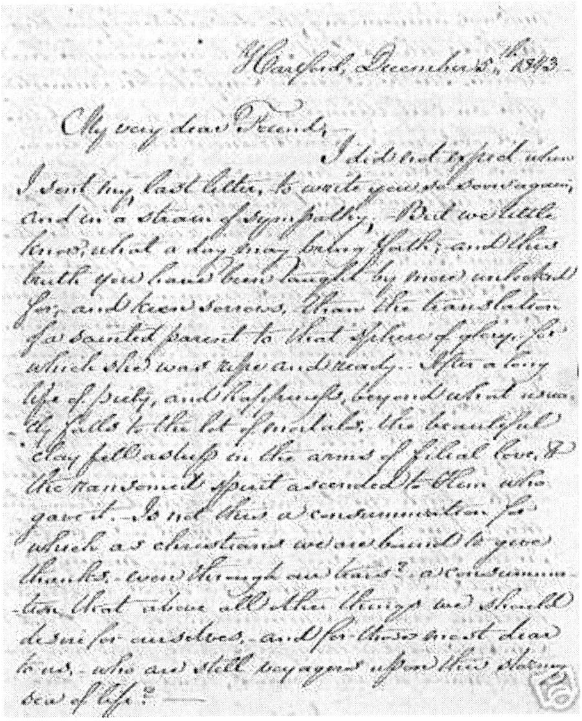

Hartford, December 5th, 1843

My very dear Friend,

I did not expect when I sent my last letter, to write you so soon again, and in a strain of sympathy. But we little know, what a day may bring forth; and this truth you have been taught by more unlooked for, and keen sorrows, than the translation of a sainted parent to that sphere of glory, for which she was ripe and ready. After a long life of piety, and happiness, beyond what usually falls to the lot of mortals, the beautiful clay fell asleep in the arms of filial love, & the ransomed spirit ascended to Him who gave it. Is not this a consummation for which as christians we are bound to give thanks, even through our tears? a consummation that above all other things we should desire for ourselves, and for those most dear to us, who are still voyagers upon this stormy sea of life? —

In Sympathy Letter describing a funeral, datelined Hartford, Connecticut, Dec 5 1843, from Lydia H. Sigourney, the important 19th century American woman author and women's education advocate, to Mrs. Sarah P. Baldwin (on the death of her mother), Care of James F. Baldwin, Tremont Street, Boston, Massachusetts with red lightly struck Hartford CT, Dec 5 postmark, red manuscript 6c postal rate.

The letter reads, in part, as follows,

> I did not expect, when I sent my last letter, to write you so soon again; and in a strain of sympathy; but we little know what a day may bring forth, and this truth you have been taught by some unlocked for, and keen sorrows, that the translation of a sainted parent to that sp of glory, for which she was ripe and ready. After a long life of piety, and happiness, beyond what usually falls to the lot of mortals, the beautiful clay fell asleep in the arms of filial love, & the ransomed spirit ascended to them who gave it. Is not this a consummation for which as Christians we are bound to give thanks, even through our tears? A consummation that above all other things we should desire for ourselves, and for those most dear to us, who are still voyagers upon this stormy sea of life?
>
> It was only yesterday evening that I received a message announcing the departure of your blessed mother. When I last sent to inquire after her health, she was quite comfortable. Immediately after an early dinner, I went over to attend the last obsequies. Dear Francis received me in the most affectionate manner. She is suffering from influenza, and not able to go out & Dr. Fuller is giving her quieting remedies for the nervous system. What a model of filial devotion has she been, to the last moment other parents' existence.
>
> She spoke with gratitude of the easy and peaceful manner in which is had pleased God to remove her dear mother, and requested me, as she could not herself go out, to take her place & walk with her dear brother. Thus I felt it a privilege to do, for the marked affection with which the departed one had always treated me, led me to regard her almost as a mother. In the church, were many wonderful friends. Dr. Spring made a most excellent & touching prayer, commending to the kind compassion of a merciful Father, those who 'were now made doubly orphans,' and giving due honour to the memory of the dead, who had died in the Lord, for, said He" She hath been a succorer of many, and of us also:
>
> 'How soothing are the offices of our holy religion, when the dust returneth unto dust". As I followed that revered form, with your able brother, I remembered you, my dear friend -- and trusted that God would give you strength to glorify Him, with a quiet spirit, under every visitation.

Your brother's little children, with their sweet, serious faces, conducted throughout the whole scene, with perfect propriety, their Mother being confined with a young infant, could not be present."

I understand that she was comfortable, though somewhat feeble. Your Aunt Williams sat with us, in your sister's room, and attended the funeral and Judge William & Mr. Parsons came over from Hartford. Maria Olmsted staid with dear Frances, and I am going to send over this afternoon to know how she—and all are. I thought these particulars would be interesting to you, dear friend & so have written them amid haste & interruptions. I know ou will strive to be submissive & thankful & may the Spirit of all grace be your aid & consolation. My best love to your good husband ... [P.S.] ... Since writing the above, I have heard from East Hartford. Your sister is comfortable, but dreads everything like excitement, and is trying to keep perfectly quiet. Let me therefore beg, if you come on, that you will make my house your home, as the meeting with one so dear, she think would be too trying to her feelings.

Lydia Sigourney was an extremely popular American poetess during the early and mid 19th century. She was commonly known as the "Sweet Singer of Hartford". Her strong beliefs were reflected in her writings.

# *Recollections of Six Days Journey in the Moon* by an Aerio-Nautical Man

The story 'Recollections of Six Days Journey in the Moon' appeared in the ***Southern Literary Messenger*** p434-437, July 1844 and was probably inadvertently influenced by a series of six articles published in the New York Sun, The Great Moon Hoax beginning August 25, 1835, it was about the supposed discovery of life and even civilization on the Moon. The discoveries were falsely attributed to Sir John Herschel, perhaps the best-known astronomer of his time.

Poe had published his own Moon hoax in late June 1835, two months before the similar Locke Moon hoax, in the Southern Literary Messenger entitled "Hans Phaall A Tale", later republished as "The Unparalleled Adventure of One Hans Pfaall".

The story was reprinted in the New York Transcript on September 2-5, 1835 under the headline "Lunar Discoveries, Extraordinary Aerial Voyage by Baron Hans Pfaall." The story is regarded as one of the first science fiction stories. Poe described a voyage to the moon in a hot-air balloon using a factually plausible scenario. Pfaall lived for five years on the Moon with lunarians and sent back a lunarian to earth. The Poe Moon hoax was less successful because of the satiric and comical tone of the account, as Poe was Editor in 1844 of the Southern Literary Messenger.

Excerpts from; ***Recollections of Six Days Journey in the Moon***. (Published in the ***Southern Literary Messenger*** – July 1844):

> Inasmuch as this terrestial world of ours has lately been so thoroughly explored by all sorts of ingenius and inquisitive travellers, who have left nothing for those that may come after them either to describe or invent, it has happened that those who, like myself are fond of new sights and new sensations, can find little or nothing here below to awaken their wonder or produce any excitement.

Even the remotest regions of the earth have been so thoroughly explored, that it may be said with perfect truth, of my countrymen most especially, that they are more intimately acquainted with the interior of Asia and Africa than the land of their birth., and know a great deal more about Paris, London, Florence and Rome, than any of our great emporiums.

Being a devoted lover of travelling, partly on account of the agreeable dissipation of mind it produces, but more especially the dignity and consequence derived from breathing the air of foreign lands. I have been seriously aggrieved at this lamentable exhaustion of novelty, and more than once, like Alexander, sat down and wept that there are no more worlds to explore.

The planets and other heavenly bodies most especially attracted my attention, and those of the Moon, which is at the bottom of so many sublunary influences, and without whose aid the adepts of Natural Philosophy would be so often at a loss to account for various phenomena, appeared to me the most interesting.

I wished, if possible, to ascertain the fact of such influence, and the mode in which it is exercised on the tides, the growth of grain and vegetables, and above all, the wits of mankind; and I was anxious for an intercourse with the Man in the Moon, who from his great age, and other collateral circumstances must, notwithstanding the perpetual insinuations about his ignorance, have acquired a prodigious mass of knowledge and experience. In short, I became exceedingly unhappy at that mysterious non-intercourse which it seemed had rendered eternal between the different planets, and to tell the honest truth, nearly lost my wits in devising expedients to surmount it, by applying some of the new principles of science to this interesting object.

While in this painful state of mind, I accidentally saw in one of the public papers a notice of some ingenious experiments in a new and hitherto unknown science, called Aeriotism, or the faculty of self-suspension in the air. It immediately occurred to me that I might convert this interesting discovery to my purpose, and pursuing the hint, I instituted a series of experiments which finally resulted in complete success, and enabled me to accomplish my long cherished object of ***a visit to the Moon, from which I have returned*** after a most refreshing tour of six days, five hours and forty seven minutes.

No time has been lost in laying the results of this journey before the enlightened public, of late so surfeited with all kinds of fictions, that it must needs feel a desire for a little wholesome truth, if only for the sake of novelty. I can not but flatter myself the information communicated will be entirely new, as hitherto we have known. Nothing of this planet, except from Astronomers and anonymous scribblers; of the former of whom I wish to speak with all possible respect, but who must be permitted to say, have told some strange stories about volcanoes and what not. As to the latter, I pledge my word to my readers I am the first native of this world who ever visited that planet, without losing his wits irrevocably; and that these egregious romancers know no more of the subject, than divers of those English travellers who have deluded mankind with pretended accounts of their discoveries and inventions, know this country.

A Trip to the Moon (French: Le Voyage dans la lune), 1902 French black and white silent science fiction film.

It is not my intention to disclose the process and final success of my experiments in Aeriotism inasmuch as I contemplate extending my visits to all the other planets in succession, and do not wish to be forestalled by others, since it can not be doubted that were I to divulge the secret, they would all in a short time be overrun by inquisitive Englishmen, who, according to custom, would leave the poor people scarcely a remnant of character, especially, as judging by those of the moon, they are far more refined, polite, moral and intelligent than those of that country, and withal better fed and more comfortable.

It will be sufficient, I trust, to insure the utmost confidence in my veracity, merely to state, as a basis of my process, that I followed the example of the aforesaid travellers, more especially the renowned "Boz," in procuring through the exertions of my numerous friends and admirers, divers public demonstrations of admiration, and a prodigious number of complimentary notices, whereby I at length became so puffed up with self-conceit, that I grew specifically lighter than the air, and felt just as I have sometimes done in my sleep, when dreaming of flying over the heads of my fellow creatures with a pair of imaginary wings. I became so light and airy, that I could not keep my feet to the ground without great difficulty, and was once blown across Cayuga Lake by a sudden gust of wind.

I was fain to wear heavy leaden soles to my boots, by means of which, though sometimes blown down, like the little witches bought by children at the toy-shops, I always popt (sic) up again in an instant, my head being so much lighter than my heels. Having thus surmounted the great obstacle of specific gravity, the next difficulty was to propel myself forward and above all govern my motions while in progress through the air. I succeeded beyond my most sanguine anticipations, by an ingenius application of machinery and mesmerism, which I shalll keep a profound secret, lest future travellers should follow in my track, and contradict all I say, as they are apt to do, in order to appear wiser than their betters.

Having perfected my machinery, and furnished myself with a bladder bag of a whip-syllabub, the ***lightest*** food I could think of, together with a map of the moon, and some cheap publications to supply me with ***light*** reading by the way, I left this world, on the night of the sixth full Moon, in the year 1844, When there was not a cloud in the sky and the air was calm, and commenced my ***daring undertaking***.

The first step, I found was everything; I rose slowly and with great difficulty, until gradually receeding from the attraction of the earth, I was borne along with such inconceivable swiftness, that I had not provided against the contingency, by an ingenious process of shortening sail, I should have left my breath behind me. As I rose in the air, I also found the great advantage of the Bozzian process I had undergone, for had not my head been already as light as a feather, I should inevitably have become so dizzy in looking down from such a fearful height, that I might probably have lost all conciousness, or at least become totally incapable of distinguishing truth from falsehood.

For the same reason that I have explained the minutiae of my machinery, I shall refrain from all detail of the particulars of my journey through the air, the dangers I encountered and my expedients for avoiding them. It is suficient to my purpose at present, merely to state, that after having encountered a vast deal of difficulty in crossing the milky way, where the stars are as close together as the thousand islands in the St. Lawrence and having my whiskers scorched by too near an approach to the Dog star, I proceeded on at a great rate, but was much alarmed to find that the Moon sailed much faster than I did, and seriously contemplated lying in her track and awaiting her coming round again.

Fortunately however, while debating the subject, I suddenly found myself rapidly approaching the land, and just at the dawn of day distinctly heard the cocks crowing. In a few minutes I was so near, as to be obliged to shorten sail, and immediately landed, where I found the Moon, like a fly in a spider web, so entangled in the beard of the comet which was marauding through the skies about this time, that she could not budge an inch. Had it not been for this providential circumstance, I verily believe I should never have overtaken her.

I had almost forgot to mention having been nearly demolished by a falling star which just grazed my head, and gave a great light, but no heat that I could discover. It may be proper also to state that I reached The Moon in two days and ten hours, in consequence of its being caught by the beard of the comet, being exactly half the time it would take , according to the calculations of Astronomers, for the planet to fall to the earth, if let go suddenly. Admitting then, that the Moon was arrested half way on her nightly course.

I must have travelled at a pretty good rate, to overtake her in so short a period. As this planet is said to be unequal in its motions, it is possible however it did not travel at this time as fast as usual.

Having a great deal of business on hand, as I contemplated a visit to the other planets, and had but little time to do it in. I determined to proceed in my inquiries into the state of the country and the character of its inhabitants without delay. Accordingly, availing myself of that facility of locomotion, I had acquired

By applying the principles of Aeriotism to practical purposes, I managed in the course of six days, to distance all previous travellers, even those who have heretofore visited my own country, and become miraculously acquainted with its morals, manners, institutions and governments, as it were by intuition.

Beginning with the geography of the country, I shall content myself with stating that the map of the Moon I carried with me, and which exhibited all the latest discoveries in the science of astronomy, is extremely inaccurate in many essential particulars. The physiognomy of this planet strikingly resembles the human face on a great scale, and hence doubtless the vulgar error of the Man in the Moon, who I assure my readers is only a creature of the imagination. The sockets of the eyes are two large seas, and the protuberances of the cheek bones and nose, nothing more than high mountains, one of the latter of which, having a reddish appearance, has doubtless been mistaken for a volcano by the astronomers.

I pledge my word, there is no such thing as a volcano in the whole planet. I had also occasion to notice that the portion of the moon which astronomers call the land is water, and their water good solid terra firma. Numerous other blunders have been committed, which I forbear to notice out of respect for the learned.

The Moon comprises several states and kingdoms, the former republican, the latter generally though not always despotic. These mutually abhor each other, and are perpetually quarrelling, and not infrequently falling together by the ears, about which is the most enlightened and happy, or other matters still more difficult to decide. Or still more insignificant.on one occasion I found two nations cutting each other's throats most valiantly, and mutually desolating fields and habitations without mercy. On inquiring the occasion of this violent animosity, I found the people knew nothing at all about it, except they were ordered to do so by their respective sovereigns, one of whom was an infant, the other a madman.

On another part of the Moon. I found them at loggerheads about the honor and interests of the country, concerning which scarcely any two agreed in opinion; or rather, there were two parties who differed altogether on the subject, one maintaining that the honor of the nation consisted altogether in its interests, the other that the interests of the nation consisted entirely on its honor. I was not a little struck with the resemblance I observed in these and many other particulars between the inhabitants of the earth and those of the Moon, which at first I ascribed to that family likenesss which is found in all creatures of the same species. Further inquiries have however satisfied me, that the people of the Moon are the genuine descendants of Adam and Eve, and that their ancestors were certainly accomplices in erecting the Tower of Babel, the proofs and deductions through which I arrived at this conclusion. I shall, however, reserve for a separate dissertation

The most remarkable kingdom in this planet, I found to be an island, called the Isle of Engines, in what is vulgarly supposed to be the left eye of the Man in the Moon, which, as I observed before, it is a great sea of salt water. It is not so large as some of the states, but has extended its dependencies to the utmost bounds of the great ocean in which it lies. I heard so much of it, at every step in my progress, that I became extremely anxious to pay it a visit and accordingly took the first opportunity that offered, embarking on a magnetic steamboat, which progressed at the rate of an hundred miles an hour, against winds and currents.

Touching this word, Progressed, I would observe that is in general use among all classes, is incorporated with all their dictionaries, and recognized as legitimate by the most learned and illustrious of all their academies, which is exclusively composed of persons who have lost their wits in searching for the Philosopher's Stone, Perpetual Motion, the wisdom of Congress, and the first principles of Political Economy.

This island which is called by its inhabitants the most free, happy and enlightened of all the countries of the Moon, I found not a little worthy the study of an enlightened traveler. Everything is done there by machinery; and the men themselves, if not machines, are as much their slaves, as the genius of Aladdin's lamp. These machines have in a great measure taken the place of men, and snatched the bread from their mouths, because they work so much cheaper and faster. I saw several which I was assured by the proprietor of a manufactory who was reckoned worth millions, could do the work of a thousand men. I asked what became of the thousand men in the meantime; upon he entered into a long dissertation to prove, that they were infinitely benefited by the cheapness of everything occasioned by these labor-saving machines.

I took the liberty of observing that the capital of a large portion of mankind was labor; and that if they could get no work, or were deprived of its adequate rewards, it was of little consequence to them that things were cheap, as they would have no money to purchase them. The millionaire looked at me with surprise, mingled as I thought with contempt and answered rather superciliously, "my good friend, I perceive you don't understand the first principles of Political Economy." I acknowledged my ignorance, and begged him to enlighten me; whereupon, he went on to entangle himself in a web of knotty arguments, sufficient to confound the whole universe, but by which he imagined that he had demonstrated his whole theory. "You see," concluded he, "the thing is as clear – as clear as"- "mud," said I, perceiving he halted for a comparison.

Believing, however, in the truth of the old proverb, "that the proof of the pudding is in the eating," I determined to see a little further into this matter; so I left the Political Economist, and proceeded through various departments of his immense establishment, where I found hundreds, I might also say, thousands of men, women and children, male and female, employed in tending machinery. They could not be said to govern but to be directed by it; and it seemed that their very souls had transmigrated into the Steam Engines and Spinning Jennies.

There were a great many female children, not more than seven or eight years old, half-clothed, and, if I might judge from their wretched squalid appearance, less than half-fed, but who, as I understood, labored sixteen or eighteen hours of the day, at this monotonous employment, which seemed to consist in perpetual watchfulness, and all for a pittance which I am afraid to name, lest no one should believe me. As I stood contemplating the scene the millionaire came suddenly behind me, and said, "ah !-Mr.-Mr.-I forget your name- I think you said you came from the United States. I think I have heard of such a place some where or other, though I can't tell where. They say it is a big country almost as big as this; but it is a great pity they tolerate slavery there.

Now, in this free and happy land, there is no such thing as a slave. The moment a man, woman, or child touches this sacred soil of freedom, the chains fall from their limbs, and they stand redeemed, regenerated and disenthralled by the irresistible genius of universal emancipation." At this moment of sublime exultation, it happened that a little pale emaciated girl, apparently worn out with toil and hunger, or both, was observed asleep, as she was standing watching the evolutions of a Spinning Jenny. Upon this a fellow came up and pinched her until she awoke with a scream, and the millionaire directed that a deduction of three pence should be made from her wages, which, on inquiry, I found amounted to two shillings a week.

I had the curiosity to follow a family to their home. It consisted of the husband, his wife, and three children, two of them girls, neither apparently over ten years of age. They had labored eighteen hours a day for months past. Yet returned to a wretched home, where two other families beside themselves lived in the same room. The weather was cold, yet they were without fire and almost destitute of any other clothing than dirty rags; their food was of the most miserable kind, and entirely insufficient to satisfy the cravings of hunger; a wretched straw bed lay in one corner, when they had eaten their scanty meal, they laid themselves down altogether, supplying the want of covering by a mutual communication of animal heat.

Turning from the scene in sickening disgust, mingled with indignation, I proceeded towards my lodgings, when I was attracted by a concourse of splendid equipages, before the doors of a great public building, into which a considerable number of people were entering. Prompted by curiousity, I followed the crowd into a splendid hall, where I found a large assemblage of distinguished persons, who, as I soon learned, were holding a meeting to raise funds for some philanthropic society, whose name I forget, but whose object was enlightening the minds or relieving the necessities of people somewhere at the antipodes.

A Royal Duke, as I afterwards learned, presided on the occasion, and a most eloquent address was delivered, in which the orator lauded the philanthropy of his country to the skies, and praised the illustrious individuals there met together, for their munificent liberality. After this, several thousand pounds were subscribed; the meeting broke up and I observed that as ***his Royal Highness*** came forth, a family similar in wretchedness, ignorance and poverty to that I have described, begged his charity. But he had done enough for one day' he had got his name before the public as a Prince of unparalled humanity, and passed on muttering something about the poor rates. For my part, I honestly confess, that I went away with my respect for that much calumniated maxim about charity beginning at home, greatly increased.

I look upon ***this island*** to be the best study on the Moon, for a politician, a philosopher, and a philanthropist; but the desire to anticipate other travelers who may possibly find their way to that planet and forestall my work, obliges me to curtail it in many interesting particulars, which I may probably supply in a future edition. At present I shall only say, that while this nation pretends to be the freest under the sun, it abounds in a species of slaves more abjectly wretched by far than those of any other country; that while it affects to take precedence of the rest of the world in learning, science and knowledge, a large portion of the people of all ages are in the state of most unparalled ignorance; that while its power and glory are said to have reached far above all that have gone before it, such are the discontents of the people that laws can only be executed by a military force; and that finally while boasting of its happiness, it comprises a portion of actual misery, greater than that of any other nation of the Moon or the Earth.

## Note

Obviously this story is allegorical and has nothing to do with the Moon. The condition of the workers could relate to either the United States or to Britain during the Industrial Revolution which commenced in the 1840's (when this article was written). Hints of a ***Military solution*** makes one think that this allegory could be an early piece of the puzzle that eventually played out over sixteen years later as the Civil War. It could also relate to the workers in Britain, who endured these same conditions in the 1840's when this article was written. – ***Robert D. Morritt***

# LOUISE ANTOINE GODEY

Louis Godey was born to French emigrant parents who were survivors of the French revolution in New York City, June 6.1804. He died in Philadelphia November 29. 1878. As immigrants they were poor. Godey did not attend school and became self-educated. He became a paper boy at the age of 15 and worked for a New York newspaper after saving his earnings he moved to Philadelphia and worked as a "scissors editor," for Charles Alexander on the ***Daily Chronicle***. Two years later he published his first Lady's Book.

Using his new editing skills his book contained article clippings from French publications. In 1830 he became the joint founder in 1830 of the ***Lady's Book*** (after his partner left it was renamed ***Godey's Lady's Book***). It became America's first successful women's magazine. The release of the ***Lady's Book*** would make Godey "the guiding star of female education, the beacon light of refined taste, pure morals, and practical wisdom." It featured articles by famous authors and colored plates of the latest fashions and etiquette, along with receipts, patterns, house plans, crafts, helpful hints, health advice, short stories, poetry, book notices, and musical scores all designed to inform "women" how to be "ladies." Ladies were also given style ideas and what type of clothing was popular at the time.

One main reason for the magazine to be the first successful woman's magazine in the United States was the hiring of Sarah Josepha Hale as the magazine's ***literary editor***. Godey hired Hale to write about the importance of advanced education for young women. Hale was also the author of the famous poem "Mary's Lamb."

Others who contributed to the magazine were Eliza Leslie, William Cullen Bryant, Harriet Beecher Stowe, and Nathaniel Hawthorne. With popularity came success. He soon became wealthy and shortly after opened up his own magazine company. The ***Godey's Lady's Book*** continued to be successful throughout the years. On August 31, 1833, Godey married Maria Duke and during their marriage they had five children together. After over ten years of success of the ***Lady's Book***, he published the

***Lady's Musical Library*** (1842) and ***The Young People's Book*** (1841). These both brought useful and entertaining knowledge to readers, but weren't quite as popular as ***Godey's Lady's Book.***

Success came at a time when the United States felt inferior to the European Continent, especially when it came to fashion. He is quoted in the ***History of American Magazines*** as saying, after retiring from the ***Lady's Book***, "that not an immoral thought or profane word could be found in its pages during the entire period of his connection with it."

Glenda Riley writes in her article, ***Origins of the Argument***, that "many of Godey's employees found him to be considerate, conservative, and a generous friend throughout the years." Publishing a successful periodical for the elevation of American "womanhood" was his great adventure. He retired to St. Augustine, FL and shortly became ill. Godey died in Philadelphia November 29, 1878, reading Anne of Geirstein in his favorite armchair. Godey lived throughout a rough period of American history but he brought forth woman's fashion and ladylike He also owned a publishing house that produced such works as ***The Young People's Book or Magazine of Useful or Entertaining Knowledge*** (1841) and the ***Lady's Musical Library*** (1842). Godey was a pioneer of fashion and of American culture mirrored in each of his highly popular women's magazines.

## Sources

Mott, Frank Luther. ***A History of American Magazines***. Cambridge, MA: Harvard UP, 1938.

Sherrer, Grace. "French Culture as Presented to Middle-Class America by Godey's Lady's Book." ***American Literature*** 3.3 (1931): 277-286. (Partial biography)

# JOHN HOWARD PAYNE

John Howard Payne was born in New York City on June 9, 1791, he was a descendant of Robert Treat Payne, one of the signers of the Declaration of Independence. After his birth the family move to Boston they also spent some time at his grandfather's colonial-era house in East Hampton, New York. The house was later preserved in Payne's honour. He displayed strong dramatic talent as a youth but his father discouraged Payne from following that as a career. When he was only thirteen after the death of an older brother he took over the late brother's position at an accountant's firm in New York.

After Payne's father's death, the English tragedian George Frederick Cooke came to America and became interested in the young actor, appearing with him in ***King Lear*** at New York's Park Theatre. He encouraged Payne to go to London for its theatre world, which he did in February 1813. Payne's first engagements as an actor in London were very successful, and he played at Drury Lane and Covent Garden theatres. Payne also went to Paris, where he attended much theater and met people within theatrical circles.

He decided to try writing, which he found he could do quite easily and quickly, in English, and translating from French to English. He was paid to translate several French plays for production in London. In 1818 he wrote his own play ***Brutus***, which he sold. Wanting to branch out, he produced some of his own pieces at Sadler's Wells Theatre, but as a theater manager, struggled to make ends meet.

In 1823 Payne worked on a play proposal with Charles Kemble, the manager of Covent Garden Theatre, out of a number he sold to him as a group for £230. Because the one Kemble chose was being produced elsewhere, Payne easily changed the plot, added lyrics for songs and duets to it, and transformed it into an opera he called ***Clari; or the Maid of Milan.*** This included his poem and ballad "***Home, Sweet Home***",
Sir Henry Bishop wrote the music, based on an Italian folk song.

When the song was published separately, it quickly sold 100,000 copies. The publishers made a considerable profit from it, net £2100 in the first year, and the producer of the opera did well. Only Payne did not really profit by its success "While his money lasted, he was a prince of bohemians", but had little business sense. While in Europe, Payne was reportedly romantically infatuated with Mary Shelley, the author of *Frankenstein*. She had nothing but a literary interest in him. Payne never married.

## "Home Sweet Home"

"Home, Sweet Home" was performed first on May 8th 1823 as part of the score and first sung by Maria Tree. Payne introduced the song at the York and Birmingham festivals in 1832. Payne later recalled that there were times when he would be in one of the cities of Europe without a penny to his name and he would hear "Home, Sweet Home," being played by organ grinders in the streets. The song's fame came many years later when two singers added it to their repertoire, Jenny Lind and Adelina Patti, added it to their concerts. Jenny Lind[1] on her record breaking tour of America used it as her closing number in her American concerts.

### *HOME, SWEET HOME*

'Mid pleasures and palaces though we may roam,
Be it ever so humble, there's no place like home;
A charm from the sky seems to hallow us there,
Which, seek through the world, is ne'er met with elsewhere.
Home, home, sweet, sweet home!
There's no place like home, oh, there's no place like home!

An exile from home, splendor dazzles in vain;
Oh, give me my lowly thatched cottage again!
The birds singing gaily, that come at my call --
Give me them -- and the peace of mind, dearer than all!
Home, home, sweet, sweet home!
There's no place like home, oh, there's no place like home!

[1] He was invited to the White House by President Filmore to hear Jenny Lind give a performance. Miss Lind sang her last number "Home, Sweet Home" directly to Mr. Payne on that occasion.

I gaze on the moon as I tread the drear wild,
And feel that my mother now thinks of her child,
As she looks on that moon from our own cottage door
Thro' the woodbine, whose fragrance shall cheer me no more.
Home, home, sweet, sweet home!
There's no place like home, oh, there's no place like home!

How sweet 'tis to sit 'neath a fond father's smile,
And the caress of a mother to soothe and beguile!
Let others delight mid new pleasures to roam,
But give me, oh, give me, the pleasures of home.
Home, home, sweet, sweet home!
There's no place like home, oh, there's no place like home!

To thee I'll return, overburdened with care;
The heart's dearest solace will smile on me there;
No more from that cottage again will I roam;
Be it ever so humble, there's no place like home.
Home, home, sweet, sweet, home!
There's no place like home, oh, there's no place like home!

***Words***; John Howard Payne
***Music***; Sir Henry Bishop

After spending nearly twenty years in Europe, Payne returned to New York and the United States in 1832. his friends arranged a benefit concert in New York to try to help him give him a stake He also toured the country with artist John James Audubon. ***Payne developed a strong interest in the Cherokee Indians***, whose fate had become a public issue. Acknowledged as one of ***the Five Civilized Tribes.***

In 1836 Payne went to Georgia as the guest of the Cherokee Chief John Ross, who opposed removal. There were great tensions within the tribe and state at the time. Major Ridge supported removal. Payne visited with Ross to collect and record the myths, religious traditions, foodways and other aspects of the Cherokees.

Payne reported his findings in popular newspaper articles, and also had considerable work that was never published. Payne's collected, unpublished papers from the 1830s have served as important source material for scholars. The writer had visited with the nation as it was on the verge of dramatic change.

In 1838 most of the Cherokee did go west on the Trail of Tears. Removal meant the Cherokee Nation was split and ransformed, with eastern and western groups developing independently after that time.

Payne believed his research demonstrated that the Cherokee were one of the Ten Lost Tribes of ancient Israel. He was reflecting contemporary historians and other researchers who still theorized this old theory in the nineteenth century. At that time when historians tried to correlate their ideas with the Bible and classical texts, and were trying to fit the Native Americans into a biblical origin. Some scholars criticized Payne ***for his refusal to accept that Cherokees had their origins in North America.*** Others considered his work biased by his attempt to show the "Hebrew" origins of Cherokee religion. When coming upon elements he seemed to recognize from Judaism, rather than seeing these as organic forms that could have arisen independently in numerous religions (Eliade), Payne ***claimed they were derived from Judaism.***

The Portuguese traveller Antonio de Montezinos brought back reports that ***some of the Lost Tribes were living among the Native Americans of the Andes in South America.*** In response to this, Manasseh ben Israel, a noted rabbi of Amsterdam, wrote on December 23, 1649:... I think that the Ten Tribes live not only there ... but also in other lands scattered everywhere; these never did come back to the ***Second Temple*** and they keep till this day still the Jewish Religion.

The work of archaeologists, linguists and anthropologists has confirmed that ***Cherokee were descended from prehistoric indigenous peoples of North America.*** Scholars have concluded that these prehistoric peoples originated from eastern Asia and migrated across the Bering Straits to North America more than 15,000 years ago. Although Payne's theory of Cherokee origins related to Biblical tribes has been replaced by the facts of Asian origin, his unpublished papers are useful to researchers as a rich source of information on the culture of the Cherokee in the early decades of the 19th century.

In 1842 President John Tyler appointed Payne as the American Consul in Tunis. He died in Tunis in 1852 and was buried there in St. George's Protestant Cemetery.

# ZEBULON PIKE

Pike was born in Lamberton, New Jersey, January 5, 1779, now a part of Trenton. His father, also named Zebulon Pike, was an officer in the Continental Army under General George Washington and served in the United States Army after the end of the Revolutionary War. The younger Pike grew to adulthood in a series of Midwestern outposts — the frontier of the United States at the time — in Ohio and Illinois. He joined his father's regiment as a cadet in 1794, earned a commission as ensign in 1799 and a first lieutenancy later that year. Pike married Clarissa Harlow Brown in 1801 and continued his military career in logistics and payroll at a series of frontier posts. His career was taken up by General James Wilkinson, who had been appointed Governor of the Upper Louisiana Territory. In 1805, Wilkinson ordered Zebulon Pike to find the source of the Mississippi River.

Zebulon Montgomery Pike Jr. was an American soldier and explorer for whom Pikes Peak in Colorado is named. His Pike expedition, mapped much of the southern portion of the Louisiana Purchase. United States

Army Captain Zebulon Pike led the ***Pike expedition*** (July 15, 1806 – July 1, 1807) to explore the south and west of the Louisiana Purchase. Roughly contemporaneous with the Lewis and Clark Expedition, Pike's excursion was the first American effort to explore the western Great Plains and the Rocky Mountains in Colorado, and marked the discovery of Pikes Peak.

## Exploration

Pike's orders were sent by General James Wilkinson[1] on June 24, 1806. Pike left Fort Bellefontaine near St. Louis, Missouri on July 15 with a

---

[1] James Wilkinson (March 24, 1757 – December 28, 1825) was an American soldier and statesman, Heersies. He served in the Army in the American Revolutionary War, but ***was twice compelled to resign***. Appointed governor of Louisiana Territory in 1805 commanded two unsuccessful campaigns in the St. Lawrence theater during the War of 1812. After his death, he was discovered to have been ***a paid agent of the Spanish Crown.***

detachment of 20 soldiers and 50 freed Osage prisoners. They followed the Missouri River and Osage River to the Osage Nation village at the present-day border of Kansas and Missouri. There, on August 15th, they returned the hostages and parleyed with the natives. Striking northwest, the group made for the Pawnee territory on the Republican River in southern Nebraska. At the Pawnee village on September 29, Pike met with the Pawnee council and announced the new protectorship of the United States government over the territory. ***He instructed them to remove a Spanish flag*** and to fly the Stars and Stripes instead.

The expeditionary force then turned south and struck out across the prairie for the Arkansas River. They reached the river on October 14, and the party split in two. One group, under Lieutenant James Biddle Wilkinson, traveled downstream along the length of the Arkansas to its mouth and back up the Mississippi to St. Louis. Pike led the other group upstream, to the west, toward the headwaters.

Upon traversing the great plains, Pike said, "This vast plains of the western hemisphere may become in time as celebrated as the sandy deserts of Africa; for I saw in my route, in various places, tracts of many leagues where the wind had thrown up the sand in all the fanciful form of the ocean's rolling wave, and on which ***not a speck of vegetable matter existed.***" This ***statement may have influenced Stephen Long***, who led an expedition to the area in 1820, to label the area on his map as the "***Great American Des*****ert**".

On November 15 Pike first saw the distant mountain he called "Grand Peak", which has since been named ***Pikes Peak***. Pike made an attempt to climb the peak, hoping to get a view of the surrounding area and set it down on his maps, but the party was not equipped to achieve the 14,000-foot summit. Pike's group ascended a lesser summit nearby--likely Mount Miller which takes its name from one of the soldiers who accompanied Pike, Theodore Miller. Despite the coming winter, Pike pressed onward up the Arkansas, and on December 7 the party reached Royal Gorge, a spectacular canyon on the Arkansas at the base of the Rocky Mountains.

The party's next goal was to reach the headwaters of the Red River and head back downstream to the Mississippi and relative safety. However, the company's bearings were at this point far askew, and they made several blundering steps in an attempt to find the river. In addition, they were not equipped for a mountain expedition, nor for hard winter weather.

Heading north, the party found the South Fork of the Platte River, and following it upstream came to what they thought was the headwaters of the Red. Turning back downstream, they returned to the point at which they had left the Arkansas originally. In fact, they had executed a large, weeks-long loop.

Hungry, cold, and exhausted, the party headed south over the mountains. Several men were left behind as they dropped from exhaustion, but Pike doggedly pressed on until January 30, when he and the ten men who were still with him came to the Rio Grande at a point near Alamosa, Colorado. Pike mistook the Rio Grande for the Red River he had been seeking. Here, he built a fort and attempted to regroup the rest of his men, strewn across miles of mountains behind him.

## Capture

At this fort on February 26 Pike and his remaining men were captured[2] by Spanish soldiers from nearby Santa Fe. Arresting the party as spies – which, in many ways, they were – the Spanish collected the rest of his men that remained unrescued and marched them south. The prisoners were marched through Santa Fe, Albuquerque, and El Paso to Chihuahua, Los Coabos, the state capital. Along the way, Pike's party was treated with respect and celebrated by the Mexican locals, and Pike made careful notes of the military strength and civilian population.

Chihuahua's Governor Salcedo was unable to keep a military officer of a neighboring country, still keeping up the pretense of friendliness, incarcerated for long. He ordered the repatriation of Pike, although some of his party were kept in jail in Mexico for years.Pike and some of his party were escorted north, through San Antonio, Texas, arriving at the border with Louisiana at Natchitoches on July 1, 1807.

---

2 This is ominous, especially with Zebulon Pike's capture and being paraded through Santa Fe, El Paso which under Spanish control at that time. It is fortuitous that Pike mapped these regions, these assisted many years later during the Mexiican War. One wonders if the telegraph had been invented then, which it was not, the fate of Pike IF James Wilkinson was aware they had 'strayed' on Spanish territory!

The Spanish formally complained to the United States Department of State, but the government maintained that the party had been one of exploration only. Ironically, Pike's capture by the Spanish, and consequent travels through New Mexico, northern Mexico, and Texas gave him more information about Spanish power than his exploration could ever have done.

Pike was promoted to captain without his knowledge while on the southwestern expedition. In 1811, he was listed as Lt. Col. Zebulon M. Pike with the 4th Infantry Regiment at the Battle of Tippecanoe.[3]

He was promoted to colonel in 1812. He continued his role as a military functionary, serving as deputy quartermaster-general in New Orleans and inspector-general during the War of 1812.Pike was promoted to brigadier general in 1813.

Along with General Jacob Brown, Pike departed from a rural military outpost, Sackets Harbor, on the New York shore of Lake Ontario, for his last military campaign. On this expedition, Pike commanded combat troops in the successful attack on York[4], (now Toronto) on April 27, 1813.

---

[3] The ***Battle of Tippecanoe*** was fought on November 7, 1811, between United States forces led by Governor William Henry Harrison of the Indiana Territory (formerly of Berkeley, Virginia) and forces of Tecumseh's growing American Indian confederation led by his twin brother Tenskwatawa. In response to rising tensions with the tribes and threats of war, a United States force of militia and regulars set out to launch a preemptive strike on the headquarters of the confederacy. The battle took place outside Prophetstown, at the confluence of the Tippecanoe and Wabash Rivers. Although the United States was victorious both tactically (as they held their ground and destroyed Prophetstown by the next morning) and strategically (Tecumseh's confederacy never recovered), the win was costly. The tribes attacked with fewer men and sustained fewer casualties. The battle was the culmination of rising tensions in a period sometimes called Tecumseh's War, which continued until Tecumseh's death in 1813. In addition to serving as an important political and symbolic victory for the American forces, the Tippecanoe defeat dealt a devastating blow to Tecumseh's confederacy, which never regained its former strength. Public opinion in the United States blamed the Native American uprising on British interference. This suspicion served as a catalyst to the War of 1812, which began only six months later.

[4] Although not significant, the Author has visited Fort York, the scene of Pike's unfortunate demise and I was allowed many years ago to handle a 'Brown Bess' musket (gun) which is still held in their Armouries. I also visited Berkeley. Plantation on the James River the ancestral home of William Henry Harrison some years ago where it was mentioned that . Harrison gave his inaugral speech in

***Pike was killed by flying rocks and other debris*** when the retreating British garrison blew up its ammunition without warning as the town's surrender negotiations were going on. His body was brought by ship back to Sackets Harbor, where his remains were buried.

Although his actual journals were confiscated by the Spanish authorities, and not recovered from Mexico until the 1900s, Pike's account of his southwest expedition was published in 1810 as ***The expeditions of Zebulon Montgomery Pike to headwaters of the Mississippi River, through Louisiana Territory, and in New Spain, during the years 1805-6-***. Pike's account had a dramatic effect on the exploration of the southwest. He described the politics in Chihuahua that led to the Mexican independence movement, as well as the trade conditions in New Mexico and Chihuahua, which descriptions helped promote the development of the Santa Fe Trail.

---

the rain and served only thirty one days as President, he died of peneumonia April 4th 1841.- ***R.D.Morritt***

# SARA PAYSON WILLIS PARTON ("FANNY FERN")

**1811- 1872**

## Sara Payson Willis Parton also known as "Fanny Fern", Writer

Sara Payson Willis Parton was born in Portland, Maine, July 9.1811. Her parents were Nathaniel and Hannah Willis. The fifth of nine children. Her original name was Grata Payson her first name was given her by her Father. The family decided to call her "Sarah". Over her lifetime she had three husbands, and three daughters. As 'Fanny Fern" she wrote about the rights of women and the problems they encountered.

She attended school at 'Catherine Beecher'[1], Hartford Connecticut. Later Fern moved to Boston and contributed to her father's paper.

---

[1] This was a small probably a one room school where Catherine Beecher gave lessons. Delia Bacon attended this same school.

In 1837, she married Charles Harrington Eldridge who was a bank cashier. The marriage was a good one, one of the happier times in her life, and they had three children: Mary in 1838, Grace in 1841 and Ellen 1844. After Ellen's birth, Fern's mother died then her daughter Mary died in 1845 of brain fever. In 1846 Eldridge died of typhoid fever leaving Fern a widow with two children.

Fern received little help from her father or in-laws and to make ends meet she married Samuel P. Farrington in 1849. It was not a good marriage and Fern left in 1851. To make ends meet, Fern tried to teach and sew but never made enough money. She started writing to make an income and her first writings were short satires printed in a Boston Newspaper called the Olive Branch.

In January of 1856, Fern married James Parton. During the year 1866, Fern was diagnosed with cancer and died in 1872 in New York City. She was buried in Massachusetts at Mount Auburn cemetery.

She wrote; ***Ruth Hall*** and ***Fern Leaves from Fanny's***. Writing under the pseudonym of "Fanny Fern," Sarah Willis was one of the most successful newspaper columnists of her day. Having lost her first husband to typhoid fever and her second husband to a divorce, Willis turned to writing as a source of income in the early 1850s. In ***Fanny Fern***, Nancy A. Walker quotes an account of the young widow living in a boarding house and notes that Willis struggled to support her two daughters (14-15). Willis's timing for entering journalism was perfect. As Marion Marzolf explains in an article in the ***Dictionary of Literary Biography***, American periodicals were booming in the 1850s and 1860s, publishing light reading for the many Americans who had recently learned to read in the common schools (360). Between 1851 and 1872, Willis published a weekly column in several newspapers, as well as six collections of her columns, two novels, and three books for children.

Willis's writing brought her both income and fame. Within a year of its publication in 1853, almost 100,000 copies of ***Fern Leaves from Fanny's Port-Folio*** were sold in England and America, and Willis earned 10 cents per copy in royalties, enabling her to buy a house in Brooklyn, New York, and live comfortably. For her column in the ***New York Ledger***, she earned $100 a week, more than any other columnist was making in 1855.

Surely one reason for Willis's success is the match between her audience and subject matter. As Walker notes, most of the people who read the literary weeklies were women (25). Willis wrote about subjects that would have interested these readers, often lashing out at problems that beset the women of the time period. In an 1858 column called "A Law More Nice Than Just," she questions the arrest of a woman for wearing men's clothes and goes on to tell a humorous story of putting on her husband's clothes and going for a stroll.

In "Independence," a column apparently inspired by the celebration of Independence Day in 1859, she asks a series of rhetorical questions about what women can or cannot do in America. In other columns, she frankly addresses women's suffrage and their right to their children. At other times, Willis was less polemical, sometimes merely reminiscing about her childhood or complaining about feeling blue.

What unifies many of these columns, however, is Willis's strong sense of her audience: ordinary women who at times feel oppressed and at other times are merely depressed, wives and mothers who worry about losing their children and about managing their skirts in rainy weather. Indeed, in both content and style, Willis's columns often encourage "female bonding." Two 1851 columns, "The Model Husband" and "Aunt Hetty on Matrimony," provide fodder for commiserating about husbands and their annoying habits. "The honey-moon is as short-lived as a lucifer-match;" Aunt Hetty proclaims, "after than you may wear your wedding-dress at the wash tub, and your night-cap to meeting, and your husband wouldn't know it" (220). Willis's conversational style complements her content.

Her 1857 column "In the Dumps," for example, contains numerous interjections and exclamation points, as these sentences illustrate: "Good Gracious, hear that wind how!" "Donkey!" "Gracious, how blue I am!" "Oh, the visions I've had on haymows!" (288). Walker suggests that this aspect of Willis's style grew out of habit of writing her columns just before deadline (21), but it seems equally likely that she was simply addressing her readers in the intimate manner of talking to friends. The enormous success of Willis's column and books suggests that "Fanny Fern" had many friends, including one who, according to Margo Culley's book *A Day at a Time*, apparently named her diary after Willis's pseudonym (qtd. in Walker ix). While Willis may never have known it, it seems that at least one of Fanny Fern's friends was writing her back.

Source; By kind permission of; Canada, Mark, Professor, University of North Carolina at Pembroke "Fanny Fern (Sarah Willis)", ***Antebellum and Civil War America***. 19 December 2006.

## Family

Father: journalist Nathaniel Willis
Mother: homemaker Hannah Willis
Siblings: eight, including journalist Nathaniel Parker Willis
Husband: bank cashier Charles Harrington Eldredge
Daughters: Mary Stace, Grace Harrington, Ellen Willis
Husband: merchant Samuel P. Farrington
Husband: biographer James Parton
Major Works
***Fern Leaves from Fanny's Port-Folio***
***Ruth Hall***
Careers
homemaker
newspaper columnist
novelist

## Chronology

**1811:** born on July 9 in Portland, Maine

**1828-1829**: attends Catharine Beecher's school in Hartford, Conn.

**1837**: marries Charles Harrington Eldredge

**1838**: gives birth to daughter Mary Stace

**1841**: gives birth to daughter Grace Harrington

**1844**: mother dies

**1844**: gives birth to daughter Ellen Willis

**1845**: daughter Mary dies of brain fever

**1845**: husband, Charles, dies of typhoid fever

**1849**: marries Samuel P. Farrington

**1852**: begins publishing regular column in ***Musical World and Times***

**1853**: ***Fern Leaves from Fanny's Port-Folio***

**1853**: ***Little Ferns for Fanny's Little Friends***

**1853**: divorced from Farrington

**1854**: ***Fern Leaves***, Second Series

**1854**: ***Ruth Hall***
**1855**: agrees to write for ***New York Ledger***
**1856**: marries James Parton
**1857**: ***Fresh Leaves***
**1857**: ***The Play-Day Book***
**1863**: daughter Grace dies
**1864**: ***The New Story Book for Children***
**1868**: ***Folly As It Flies***
**1868**: helps form Sorosis, a women's press organization
**1870**: ***Ginger-Snaps***
**1872**: ***Caper-Sauce***
**1872**: dies of cancer on October 10

By kind permission of*;* Canada, Mark, Professor, University of North Carolina at Pembroke "Fanny Fern (Sarah Willis)", ***Antebellum and Civil War America***. 19th December 2006.

# HENRY TIMROD

**December 8, 1828 - October 7, 1867**

Timrod was born to a family of German descent, in Charleston, South Carolina. The name had been transposed and anglicised from the origina spelling of 'Dimroth'.His father was an officer in the Seminole Wars[1]

---

[1] In 1829, Andrew Jackson, President of the United States worked to have the Indian Removal Act passed by Congress. It became law in 1830. The purpose was to move all the Indians to land west of the Mississippi River. The Seminole ***did not want to leave their Florida home***, the chiefs were persuaded to sign a treaty agreeing to move. When they returned back to Florida, however, they claimed they had been tricked and refused to leave. A warrior named Osceola led the Seminole in surprise attacks against the Americans. The first battle of the war known as the Dade Massacre. It occurred when Major Dade led a combined Army from Fort Brooke (Tampa) and Fort King (Ocala). In an attack by Osceola and his men, over a hundred soldiers were killed near what is now Bushnell.

The United States sent many troops into Florida to defeat the Seminole. They were successful in pushing the Seminole further and further south into the wilderness. Several agreements were made by Seminole chiefs to leave the area, but the agreements continually fell through. Finally, Osceola was captured and he died in prison in 1838. Following his death, the Seminole began to decline. Many were killed; others were captured and relocated out west.

Timrod studied at the University of Georgia, but, forced by illness to end his formal studies, returned to Charleston. He took a position with a lawyer and planned to begin a law practice.

From 1848 to 1853 he submitted a number of poems to the ***Southern Literary Messenger***, under the pen name ***Aglaus***, where he attracted some attention for his abilities. Encouraged, he left the field of law for writing and tutoring. In 1856 he accepted a post as a teacher at the plantation of Col. William Henry Cannon in the area that would later become Florence, South Carolina.

The earliest edition of Timrod's poems was a small volume by Ticknor & Fields, of Boston, in 1860, just before the Civil War, even though The "New York Tribune" had announced within the first volume,: "These poems are worthy of a wide audience, and they form a welcome offering to the common literature of our country." The book was a commercial failure, but helped increase his popularity. It is stated that the best known poem in the book was ***A Vision of Poesy.***

With the outbreak of war, Henry returned to Charleston, soon publishing his best known poems, which drew many young men to enlist in the service of the Confederacy. His best known poems of the time are ***Ethnogenesis***, ***A Cry to Arms***, ***Carolina***, and ***Katie***. He was a frequent contributor of poems to ***Russell's Magazine*** and to ***The Southern Literary Messenger***.Timrod soon followed into the military as a Private in Company B, 20th South Carolina Infantry, but illness prevented much service, and he was sent home. After the bloody Battle of Shiloh, he tried again to live the camp life as a western war correspondent for the Charleston ***Mercury***, but this too was short lived as he was not strong enough for the rugged task.

He returned from the front and settled in Columbia to become associate editor of the newspaper, ***The South Carolinian***. In February 1864 he married his beloved Katie, and soon had a son, Willie, born on Christmas Eve. During the occupation by General Sherman's troops in February 1865, he was forced into hiding, and the newspaper office was destroyed. The aftermath of war brought his family poverty and to him, increasing illness.

---

On August 14, 1842, The Second Seminole War officially ended. As a result, many Seminole were sent to reservations in the west.

He took a post as correspondent for a new newspaper based in Charleston, ***The Carolinian***, but after several months of work, he was never paid, and the paper folded. His son Willie soon died, and Henry was to join him in death, of consumption in 1867. He is interred in the churchyard at Trinity Episcopal Church in Columbia, South Carolina.

Timrod's friend and fellow poet, Paul Hamilton Hayne, posthumously edited and published ***The Poems of Henry Timrod***, with more of Timrod's more famous poems in 1873, including his ***Ode: Sung on the Occasion of Decorating the Graves of the Confederate Dead at Magnolia Cemetery, Charleston, S.C., 1867*** and ***The Cotton Boll***.

Timrod is regarded as an important writer of nineteenth-century American literature. He was honoured in 1911 by the State's General Assembly who passed a resolution to officially adopt the verses of his poem "Carolina" as the lyrics of the official state anthem.

***PRÆCEPTOR AMAT***

It is time (it was time long ago) I should sever
This chain—why I wear it I know not—forever!
Yet I cling to the bond, e'en while sick of the mask
I must wear, as of one whom his commonplace task
And proof-armor of dullness have steeled to her charms!
Ah! how lovely she looked as she flung from her arms,
In heaps to this table (now starred with the stains
Of her booty yet wet with those yesterday rains),
These roses and lilies, and—what? let me see!
Then was off in a moment, but turned with a glee,
That lit her sweet face as with moonlight, to say,
As 't was almost too late for a lesson to-day,
She meant to usurp, for this morning at least,
My office of Tutor; and instead of a feast
Of such mouthfuls as 'poluphloisboio thalasses',
With which I fed her, I should study the grasses
(Love-grasses she called them), the buds, and the flowers
Of which I know nothing; and if "with MY powers",
I did not learn all she could teach in that time,
And thank her, perhaps, in a sweet English rhyme,

If I did not do this, and she flung back her hair,
And shook her bright head with a menacing air,
She'd be—oh! she'd be—a real Saracen Omar
To a certain much-valued edition of Homer!

But these flowers! I believe I could number as soon
The shadowy thoughts of a last summer's noon,
Or recall with their phases, each one after one,
The clouds that came down to the death of the Sun,
Cirrus, Stratus, or Nimbus, some evening last year,
As unravel the web of one genus! Why, there,
As they lie by my desk in that glistering heap,
All tangled together like dreams in the sleep
Of a bliss-fevered heart, I might turn them and turn
Till night, in a puzzle of pleasure, and learn
Not a fact, not a secret I prize half so much,
As, how rough is this leaf when I think of her touch.
There's one now blown yonder! what can be its name?

A topaz wine-colored, the wine in a flame;
And another that's hued like the pulp of a melon,
But sprinkled all o'er as with seed-pearls of Ceylon;
And a third! its white petals just clouded with pink!
And a fourth, that blue star! and then this, too! I think
If one brought me this moment an amethyst cup,
From which, through a liquor of amber, looked up,
With a glow as of eyes in their elfin-like lustre,
Stones culled from all lands in a sunshiny cluster,
From the ruby that burns in the sands of Mysore
To the beryl of Daunia, with gems from the core
Of the mountains of Persia (I talk like a boy
In the flush of some new, and yet half-tasted joy);

But I think if that cup and its jewels together
Were placed by the side of this child of the weather
(This one which she touched with her mouth, and let slip
From her fingers by chance, as her exquisite lip,
With a music befitting the language divine,
Gave the roll of the Greek's multitudinous line),
I should take—not the gems—but enough! let me shut
In the blossom that woke it, my folly, and put
Both away in my bosom—there, in a heart-niche,
One shall outlive the other—is 't hard to tell which?
In the name of all starry and beautiful things,
What is it? the cross in the centre, these rings,
And the petals that shoot in an intricate maze,
From the disk which is lilac--or purple? like rays
In a blue Aureole!

And so now will she wot,
When I sit by her side with my brows in a knot,
And praise her so calmly, or chide her perhaps,
If her voice falter once in its musical lapse,
As I've done, I confess, just to gaze at a flush
In the white of her throat, or to watch the quick rush
Of the tear she sheds smiling, as, drooping her curls
O'er that book I keep shrined like a casket of pearls,
She reads on in low tones of such tremulous sweetness,
That (in spite of some faults) I am forced, in discreetness,
To silence, lest mine, growing hoarse, should betray
What I must not reveal--will she guess now, I say,

How, for all his grave looks, the stern, passionless Tutor,
With more than the love of her youth-fullest suitor,
Is hiding somewhere in the shroud of his vest,
By a heart that is beating wild wings in its nest,
This flower, thrown aside in the sport of a minute,
And which he holds dear as though folded within it
Lay the germ of the bliss that he dreams of! Ah, me!
It is hard to love thus, yet to seem and to be
A thing for indifference, faint praise, or cold blame,
When you long (by the right of deep passion, the claim,
On the loved of the loving, at least to be heard)
To take the white hand, and with glance, touch, and word,
Burn your way to the heart! That her step on the stair?
Be still thou fond flutterer!

How little I care
For your favorites, see! they are all of them, look!
On the spot where they fell, and--but here is your book!

By Henry Timrod

# HENRY CLAY LEWIS – THE SWAMP DOCTOR

Henry Clay Lewis was born in Charleston, South Carolina, on June 26, 1825. He was an American short story writer and medical doctor from the middle of the 19th century.

Lewis wrote in the style of "Old Southwest Humor" for his only book, Odd Leaves from the Life of a Louisiana Swamp Doctor, which he wrote under the pseudonym ***Madison Tensas***

He was the seventh child of David and Rachel Salomon Lewis. Henry lived in Charleston only four years before his father left his furniture store there and moved the family to Cincinnati, Ohio. Rachel Lewis died shortly thereafter, which marked the beginning of Henry's tumultuous childhood. After the death of his mother he was sent to live with his older married brother, Alexander, Henry found life with him unpleasant and escaped to the Ohio River at age ten. He worked odd jobs on several ships before landing in Yazoo City, Mississippi, (then called Manchester) where he was reunited with another brother named Joseph. Henry gave up the river in hopes of finally gaining an education with funds promised by Joseph; however, his brother's financial holdings were wiped out in 1837, and Henry began working in the cotton fields instead. When he turned sixteen he apprenticed with a doctor named Washington Dorey, and in 1844 he moved to Louisville, Kentucky to enter Louisville Medical College. Later he returned to Yazoo City to open a practice which failed from lack of business. He then moved his practice to a swampy, remote area of Louisiana, Madison Parish, on the Tensas River.[1]

There he observed and participated in the very frontier life that he later incorporated into popular literary sketches featuring a young swamp doctor named Madison Tensas. Beginning in 1847, several of these were published under the pseudonym "Madison Tensas" in New York's ***Spirit of the Times.***

[1] He took his pseudonym 'Tensas" from the name of the same river.

Three years later and still a bachelor, Lewis moved to the more affluent Richmond, Louisiana, where he expanded his practice and awaited the publication of his only book, ***Odd Leaves from the Life of a Louisiana Swamp Doctor***. Reminiscent of the text's fearless physician who often braves the frontier's elements to serve his community, Henry Clay Lewis drowned on August 5, 1850 at age twenty-five, while crossing a flooded river on his way home from treating cholera patients.

There is some controversy as to when *Odd* ***Leaves from the Life of a Louisiana Swamp Doctor*** was first published. The 1858 edition, published by T. B. Peterson, depicted an original issue date of 1843 with the publishing firm Carey & Hart of Philadelphia. There is also an ***unpublished edition*** dated 1846. Most sources agree that the first viable date of publication for ***Odd Leaves*** was 1850 by, A. Hart of Philadelphia.

***Odd Leaves*** is a collection of twenty-two frontier sketches capturing the humor of the Old Southwest. This literary style, inaugurated by Augustus Baldwin Longstreet in ***Georgia Scenes*** (1835), is often characterized by regional dialect, coarse humor, and an unchecked violence associated with early American rural life. Autobiographical in many respects, ***Odd Leaves*** relays the story of a swamp doctor named "***Madison Tensas***", whose wandering childhood, medical school years, and rural Louisiana practice parallel Lewis's own upbringing and professional experience.

Lewis's humorous sketches contain a variety of humor, from farce and tall-tale hoaxes to the more grotesque. In one of the collection's earlier stories, "Getting Acquainted with the Medicines," the narrator, Madison Tensas, ridicules his own ignorance by describing how his apprenticeship with a local doctor goes awry. Believing that the doctor has told him to "digest" the contents of a medicine shelf in order to experience their effects, he duly hesitates upon realizing that the first specimen is a four-gallon jug labeled "***Arsenic: deadly poison***."

To Madison's surprise, an Indian named Old Tubba sitting on the office steps gladly volunteers to drink the solution for him. Madison turns him down, but realizes later that Old Tubba already has consumed a large quantity of the jug's contents and lies unconscious nearby.

The young doctor frantically calls on several medical students to help him diagnose the case, but their flurry of illogical speculations are put to rest when the doctor returns. He pronounces Old Tubba drunk rather than dying. As Madison learns, the doctor had cleverly hidden his stash of whiskey from all save one.

The tales include uncouth humour and tall tales as noted in, "A Tight Race Considerin'." The scenario is that of a friend's mother who challenges the local preacher to a horse race. They both then rode directly into the bushes outside the meetinghouse, where they were discovered in a compromising position. Lewis wrote, "The Indefatigable Bear-Hunter" about a man named Mik-hoo-tah, an avid hunter who lost a leg and later he killed a bear by clubbing it with his new wooden leg.

The humor of ***Odd Leaves*** contained some grotesque sketches, including "The Day of Judgment" and "Stealing a Baby." In the former, Madison and his boardinghouse roommates play a gruesome trick on their landlady in order to scare her out of her snooping habits. One evening the medical students leave wrapped in their room the face of a cadaver, and watch through the window as she once again rummages through their belongings. When she discovers the package, she hurriedly unwrapped it; however, her response is to laugh and comment that little could offend or surprise her after so many years of married life. "Stealing a Baby" incorporates similarly grisly humor as Madison describes smuggling an infant cadaver from the medical school's premises so that he can study it further in his room. Unluckily, he meets a sweetheart and her father in the street, and the awkwardness of his circumstance causes him to drop the baby in front of them.

***Odd Leaves*** contains illustrations by renowned artist, Felix Octavius Carr Darley (1822-1888), whose drawings also appeared in the works of Washington Irving, James Fenimore Cooper, and Charles Dickens. Born in Philadelphia, Lewis' sketches appeared as a collection in book form in 1850, published under the pseudonym “Madison Tensas”.

***"My cloak flew open as I fell, and the force of the fall bursting its envelope, out, in all the hideous realities, rolled the infernal imp of darkness."***

## The City Physician versus the Swamp Doctor

The city physician, or the country doctor of an old-settled locality, with all the appliances of cultivated and refined life around them; possessing all the numberless conveniences and luxuries of the sick-room; capable of controlling the many adverse circumstances that exert such a pernicious influence upon successful practice; having at command the assistance, in critical and anomalous cases, of scientific and experienced coadjutors; the facilities of good roads; the advantages of comfortable dwellings, easy carriages, and the pleasures of commingling with a cultivated, mild, refined society.

Cannot fully realize and appreciate the condition of their less favored, humble brethren, who, impelled by youthfulness, poverty, defective education, or the reckless spirit of adventure, have taken up their lot with society nearly in its primitive condition, and dispense the blessings of their profession to the inhabitants of a country, where the obscure bridle-path, the un-bridged water-courses, the deadened forest trees, the ringing of the woodman's axe, the humble log cabin, the homespun dress, and all the many sober, hard realities of pioneer life, attest the youthfulness of the settlement. The city physician may be of timorous nature and weak and effeminate constitution:

The "swamp doctor," whose midnight ride is often saluted by the scream of the panther, must be of courageous nature, and in physical endurance as hardy as one of his own grand alluvial oaks, whose canopy of leaves is many a night his only shelter.

The city physician may be of fastidious taste, and exquisiteness of feeling; the swamp doctor must have the unconcernedness of the dissecting-room, and be prepared to swallow his peck of dirt all at once.

The city physician must be of polished manners and courtly language: the swamp doctor finds the only use he has for bows, is to escape some impending one that threatens him with Absalomic fate; the only necessity for courtly expression, to induce some bellicose "squatter" to pay his bill in something besides hot curses and cold lead.

The city physician, fast anchored in the sublimity of scientific expression, requires a patient to "inflate his lungs to their utmost capacity;" the swamp doctor tells his to "draw a long breath, or swell your d--dest:" one calls an individual's physical peculiarities, "idiosyncrasy;" the other terms it "a fellow's nater." The city physician sends his prescriptions to the drug store, and gives himself no regard as to the purity of the medicine; each swamp doctor is his own ***pharmacien***, and carries his drug store at the saddle.

The city physician rides in an easy carriage over well paved streets, and pays toll at the bridge; we mount a canoe, a pair of mud boots, sometimes a horse, and traverse, unmindful of exposure or danger, the sullen slough or angry river.

The city physician wears broadcloth, and looking in his hat reads, "Paris;" we adorn the outer man with homespun, and gazing at our graceful castors remember the identical hollow tree in which we caught the coon that forms its fair outline and symmetrical proportions. The city physician goes to the opera or theatre, to relax, and while away a leisure evening. The swamp doctor resorts for the same purpose to a deer or bear hunt, a barbecue or bran dance, and generally ends by becoming perfectly hilarious, and evincing a determination to sit up in order that he can escort the young ladies home before breakfast.

The city physician, compelled to keep up appearances, deems a library of a hundred authors a moderate collection; the swamp doctor glories in the possession of "Gunn's Domestic Medicine," and the "Mother's Guide."

The city physician has a costly Parisian instrument for performing operations, and scorns to extract a tooth; the swamp doctor can rarely boast of a case of amputating instruments, and practices dentistry with a gum lancet and a pair of pullikens.

The city physician, with intellect refined, but feelings vitiated by the corruptings and heart-hardenings of modern polished society, views with utter indifference or affected sympathy the dissolution of body and soul in his patients: but think you, ***we*** can see depart unmoved those with whom we have endured privations, have been knit like brothers together by our mutual dangers; with whom we have hunted, fished, and shared the crust and lowly couch; with whom we have rejoiced and sorrowed; think you *we* can see them go down to the grave with tearless eyes, with unmoved soul?

If we can, then blot out that expression so accordant with common sentiment, "God made the country, and man the town."

The city physician sends the poor to the hospital, and eventually to the dissecting-room; we tend and furnish them gratuitously, and a proposal to dispose of them anatomically would, in all probability, put a knife into us. One, with a sickly frame, anticipates old age; the other, with a vigorous constitution, knows that exposure and privation will cut him off ere his meridian be reached.

The city physician has soft hands, soft skin, and soft clothes: we have soft hearts but hard hands; we are rough in our phrases, but true in our natures; our words do not speak one language and our actions another; what we mean we say, what we say we mean; our characters, when not original, are impressed upon us by the people we practice among and associate with, for such is the character of the pioneers and pre-emptionists of the swamp.

To sum up the whole, the city physician lives at the top of the pot, the swamp doctor scarcely at the rim of the skillet: one is a delicate carpet, which none but the nicest kid can press; the other is a cypress floor, in which the hobnails of every clown can stamp their shape: one is the breast of a chicken, the other is a muscle-shell full of cat-fish: one is quinine, the other Peruvian bark: and so on in the scale of proportions.
I have contrasted the two through the busy, moving scenes of life; let me keep the curtain from descending awhile, till I draw the last and awful contrast.

Stand by the death-bed of the two, in that last and solemn hour, when disease has prescribed for the patient, and death, acting the ***pharmacien***, is filling the R. In a close, suffocating room, horizontalized on a feather bed; if a bachelor, attended by a mercenary nurse; his departure eagerly desired by a host of expectant, envious competitors; with the noise of drays, the shouts of the busy multitude, and the many discordant cries of the city ringing through his frame, the soul of the city physician leaves its mortal tenement and wings its way to heaven through several floors and thicknesses of mortar and brick, whilst the sobs of his few true friends float on the air strangely mingled with "Pies all hot!" "The last 'erald!" and "Five dollars reward, five dollars reward, for the lost child of a disconsolate family!"

The swamp doctor is gathered unto his fathers 'neath the greenwood tree, couched on the yielding grass, with the soft melody of birds, the melancholy cadence of the summer wind, the rippling of the stream, the sweet smell of flowers, and the blue sky above bending down as if to embrace him, to soothe his spirit, and give his parting soul a glance of that heaven which surely awaits him as a recompense for all the privations he has endured on earth.

Whilst the pressure on his palm of hard and manly hands, the tears of women attached to him like a brother by the past kind ministerings of his Godlike calling, the sobs of children, and the boisterous grief of the poor negroes, attest that not unregarded or unloved he hath dwelt on earth: a sunbeam steals through the leafy canopy and clothes his brow with a living halo, a sweet smile pervades his countenance, and amidst all that is beauteous in nature or commendable in man, the swamp doctor sinks in the blissful luxuries of death; no more to undergo privation and danger, disease or suffering.

He hath given his last pill, had his last draught protested against; true to the instincts of his profession, he, no doubt, in the battling troop of the angels above, if feasible, will still continue to ***charge.***

# Edgar Allan Poe

The 'Early' Poe

A Photographic comparison of Edgar Allan Poe refecting his early energetic composure with the latter depicting a different, a fatigued, morose person consumed by his demons possibly brought on by his affliction for alcohol and years of fretting over the loss of the love of his life, Virginia Clemm, his cousin that he married when she was thirteen.

Virginia Clemm

He was born as Edgar Poe in Boston, Massachusetts; he was orphaned young when his mother died shortly after his father abandoned the family. Poe was taken in by John and Frances Allan, of Richmond, Virginia, but they never formally adopted him. He attended the University of Virginia for one semester but left due to lack of money. After enlisting in the Army and later failing as an officer's cadet at West Point, Poe parted ways with the Allans. His publishing career began humbly, with an anonymous collection of poems, ***Tamerlane and Other Poems*** (1827), credited only to "a Bostonian".

Poe switched his focus to prose and spent the next several years working for literary journals and periodicals, becoming known for his own style of literary criticism. His work forced him to move between several cities, including Baltimore, Philadelphia, and New York City. In Baltimore in 1835, he married Virginia Clemm, ***his 13-year-old cousin***.

In January 1845, Poe published his poem "The Raven" to instant success. His wife died of tuberculosis two years later. He began planning to produce his own journal, ***The Pen*** (later renamed ***The Stylus***), though he died before it could be produced. On October 7, 1849, at age 40, Poe died in Baltimore; the cause of his death is unknown and has been variously attributed to alcohol, brain congestion, cholera, drugs, heart disease, rabies, suicide, tuberculosis, and other agents.

Poe and his works influenced literature in the United States and around the world, as well as in specialized fields, such as cosmology and cryptography. Poe and his work appear

## Note

The author is cognizant of the easy accessibility of material of Edgar Allan Poe. As we are dealing with the antebellum period, it would be a fallacy for me to ignore him but, that being said, I will include a brief item of more obscurity for the general reader. 'Tamerlane' is featured herein to give an idea of his early 'style' of writing which was contemporary and similar to the Byronic school in his early years. Later his style evolved and he concentrated on the realm of detection and the macabre.

## Tamerlane and other Poems by a Bostonian

Tamerlane is the first published work by American writer Edgar Allan Poe. The short collection of poems was first published in 1827. Today, it is believed only 12 copies of the collection still exist.

Poe abandoned his foster family, the Allans, and moved to Boston to find work in 1827. Having only minor success, he enlisted in the United States Army. He brought with him several manuscripts, which he paid to have published by a printer named Calvin F. S. Thomas. The 40-page collection was called ***Tamerlane and Other Poems*** and did not include Poe's name. Distribution was limited to 50 copies and it received no critical attention. The poems were largely inspired by Lord Byron, including the long title poem "Tamerlane", which depicts a historical conqueror who laments the loss of his first romance. Like much of Poe's future work, the poems in ***Tamerlane and Other Poems*** include themes of love, death, and pride.

***TAMERLANE***

**I**

I have sent for thee, holy friar;
But 'twas not with drunken hopc,
Which is but agony of desire
To shun the fate, with which to cope
Is more than crime may dare to dream,
That I have call'd thee at this hour:
Such father is not my theme-
Nor am I mad, to deem that power
Of earth may shrive me of the sin
Unearthly pride hath revell'd in –
I would not call thee fool, old man,
But hope is not a gift of thine;
If I *can* hope (O God! I can)
It falls from an eternal shrine.

**II**

The gay wall of this gaudy tower
Grows dim around me-death is near,
I had not thought, until this hour
When passing from the earth, that car
Of any, were it not the shade
Of one whom in life I made
All mystery but a simple name,

Might know the secret of a spirit
Bow'd down in sorrow, and in shame.-
Shame said'st thou?
Aye I did inherit
That hated portion with the fame,
The world glory which has shown
A demon-light around my throne,
Scorching my sear'd heart with a pain
Not Hell shall make me fear again.

**III**

I have not always been as now-
The fever'd diadem on my brow
I claim'd and won usurpingly-
Aye- the same heritage hath giv'n
Rome to Caesar-this to me;
The heirdom of a kingly mind-
And a proud spirit which hath striv'n
Triumphantly with human kind
In mountain air I first drew life;
The mists of the Taglay have shed
Nightly their dews on my young head;
And my brain drank their venom then,
When after day of perilous strife
With chamois, I would seize his den
And slumber, in my pride of power,
The infant monarch of the hour-
For, with the mountain dew by night,
My soul imbib'd unhallow'd feeling;
And I would feel its essence stealing
In dreams upon me-while the light
Flashing from cloud that hover'd o'er,
Would seem to my half closing eye
The pageantry of monarchy!
And the deep thunder's echoing roar
Come hurriedly upon me, telling
Of war, and tumult, where my voice
My *own* voice, silly child! was swelling
(O how would my wild heart rejoice
And leap within me at cry)
The battle-cry of victory!

**IV**

The rain came down upon my head
But barely shelter'd-and the wind
Pass'd quickly o'er me-but my mind
Was mad'ning-for 'twas man that shed
Laurels upon me-and the rush
The torrent of the chilly air
Gurgled in my pleas'd ear the crash
Of empires, with the captive's prayer
The hum of suitors, the mix'd tone
Of flatt'ry round a siv'reign's throne
The storm had ceas'd- and I awoke-
Its spirit had ceas'd-and I awoke
Its spirit cradled me to sleep,
And as it pass'd me by,, there broke
Strange light upon me, tho' it were
My soul in mystery to sleep
For I was not as I had been;
The child of Nature, without care,
Or thought, dave of the passing scene.

**V**

My passions, from that hapless hour,
Usurp'd a tyranny, which men
Have deem'd, since I have reach'd to power
My innate nature-be it so;
But father, there liv'd but one who, then-
Then, in my boyhood, when their fire
Burn'd with a still intenser glow;
(For passion must with youth expire)
Ev'n *then*, who deem'd this iron heart,
In woman's weakness had a part,
I have no words, alas! to tell
The lovliness of loving well!
Nor would I dare attempt to trace
The breathing beauty of a face,
Which ev'n to *my* impassion'd mind,
Leaves not its memory behind.
In spring of life have ye ne'er dwelt
Some object of delight upon,
With steadfast eye, till ye have felt
The earth reel-and the vision gone?
And I have held to mem'rys eye,
One object-and but one-until
It's very form hath pass'd me by,
But left its influence with me still,

**VI**

'Tis not to thee that I should name-
Thou can't not-would'st not dare to think
The magic empire of a flame
Which ev'n upon this perilous brink
Hath fix's my soul, tho' unforgiv'n
By what it lost for passion-Heav'n.
I lov'd-and O, how tenderly!
Yes! she [was] worthy of all love!
Such as in infancy was mine
Tho' then its *passion* could not be;
'Twas such as angel minds above
Might envy-her young heart the shrine
On which my ev'ry hope and thought
Were incense-then a goodly gift-
For they were childish, without sin,
Pure as her young examples taught;
Why did I leave it and adrift,
Trust to the fickle star within

**VII**

We grew in age, and love together,
Roaming the forest and the wild;
My breast her shield in wintry weather,
And when the friendly sunshine smild'd
And she would mark the op'ning skies,
I saw no Heav'n, but in her eyes-
Ev'n childhood knows the human heart;
For when, in sunshine and in smiles,
From all our little cares apart,
Laughing at her half silly wiles,
I'd throw me on her throbbing breast.
And pour my spirit out in tears,
She'd look up in my wilder'd eye-
There was no need to speak the rest—
No need to quiet her kind fears-
She did not ask the reason why.
The hallow'd mem'ry of those years
Comes o'er me in these lonely hours,
And, with sweet lovliness, appears
As a perfume of strange summer flow'rs;
Of flow'rs which we have known before
In infancy, which seen, recall
To mind-not flow'rs alone-but more
Our earthly life and love-and all

**VIII**

Yes! she was worthy of all love!
Ev'n such as from th' accursed time
My spirit with the tempest strove,
When on the mountain peak alone,
Ambition lent it a new tone,
And bade it first to dream of crime,
My phrenzy[frenzy] to her bosom taught;
We still were young: no purer thought
Dwell [Dwelt] in a seraph's breast than *thine*'
For passionate love is still divine;
I lov'd her as an angel might
With ray of the all living light
Which blazes upon Edis' shrine.
It is not surely sin to name,
With such as mine-that mystic flame,
I had no being but in thee!
The world with all its train of bright
And happy beauty (for to me
All was an undefin'd delight)
The world-its joy-its share of pain
Which I felt not-its bodied forms
Of varied being, which contain
The bodiless spirits of the storms,
The sunshine, and the calm-the ideal
And fleeting vanities of dreams,
Fearfully beautifu;! the real
Nothings of mid-day waking life-
Of an enchanted life, which seems,
Now as I look back, the strife
Of some ill demon, with a power
Which left me in an evil hour,
All that I felt, or saw, or thought,
Crowding, confused became
(With thine unearthly beauty fraught)
Thou-and the nothing of a name.

**IX**

The passionate spirit which hath known
And deeply felt the silent tone
Of its own self supremacy,-
(I speak thus openly to thee,
'Twere folly *now* to veil a thought
With which this aching, breast is fraught)
The soul which feels its innate right-
The mystic empire and high power
Giv'n by the energetic might
Of Genius. at its natal hour;
Which knows (believe me at this time,
When falsehood were a ten-fold crime,
There ***is*** a power in the high spirit
To know the fate it will inherit)
The soul, which knows such power, will still
Find ***Pride*** the ruler of its will.
Yes! I was proud-and ye know who
The magic of that meaning word
So oft perverted, will bestow
Your scorn, perhaps, when ye have heard
That the proud spirit had been broken,
The proud heart burst in agony
At one upbraiding word or token
Of her that heart's idolatry-
I was ambitious-have ye known
Its fiery passion?-ye have not-
A cottager, I mark'd a throne
Of half the world, as all m y own,
And murmur'd at such lowly lot!
But it had pass'd me as a dream
Which, of light step, flies with the dew,
That kindling thught-did not the beam
Of Beauty, which did guide me through
The livelong summer day, oppress
My mind with double loveliness-

**X**

We walk'd together on the crown
Of a high mountain, which look'd down
Afar from its proud natural towers
Of rock and forest, on the hills-
The dwindled hills, whence amid bowers
Her own fair hand had rear'd around,
Gush'd shoutingly a thousand rills,
Which as it were, in fairy bound
Embrac'd two hamlets-those our own-
Peacefully happy-yet alone-
I spoke to her of power and pride-
But mystically, in such guise,
That she might deem it naught beside
The moment's converse, in her eyes
I read(perhaps too carelessly)
A mingled feeling with my own;
The flush on her bright cheek, to me
Seem'd to become a queenly throne
Too well, that I should let it be
A light in the dark wild, alone.

**XI**

There-I that hour- a thought came o'er
My mind, it had not known before-
To leave her while we both were young,-
To follow my high fate among
The strife of nations, and redeem
The idle words, which, as a dream
Now sounded to her heedless ear-
I held no doubt- I knew no fear
Of peril in my wild career;
To gain an empire, and throw down

As nuptial dowry-a queen's crown.
The only feeling which possest,
With her own image, my fond breast-
Who, that had known the secret thought
Of a young peasant's bosom then,
Had deem'd him, in compassion, aught
But one, whom phantasy had led
Astray from reason-Among men
Ambition is chain'd down-nor fed
(As in the desert, where the grand,

The wild, the beautiful, conspire
With their own breath to fan its fire)
With thoughts such feeling can command;
Uncheck'd by sarcasm, and scorn
Of those, who hardly will conceive
That any should become "great," born
In their own sphere-will not believe
That they shall stoop in life to one
Whom daily they are wont to see
Familiarly-whom Fortune's sun
Hath ne'er shone dazzlingly upon
Lowly-and of their own degree-

**XII**
I pictur'd to my fancy's eye
Her silent, deep astonishment,
When, a few fleeting years gone by;
(For short the time my high hope lent
To its most desperate intent,)
She might recall in him, whom Fame
Had gilded with a conqueror's name
(With glory-such as might inspire
Peforce, a passing thought of one,
Whom, she had deem'd in his own fire
Wither'd and blasted; who had gone
A traitor, violate of the truth
So plighted in his early youth,)
Her own Alexis, who should plight
The love he plighted ***then*** –again,
And raise his infancy's delight,
The bride and queen of Tamerlane-

**XIII**
One noon of a bright summer's day
I pass'd from out the matted bow'r
Where in a deep, still slumber lay
My Ada, In that peaceful hour,
A silent gaze was my farewell.
I had no solace-then
T'awake her, and a falsehood tell
Of a feign'd journey, were again
To trust the weakness of my heart
To her soft thrilling voice;To part

Thus, haply, while in sleep she dream'd
Of long delight, nor yet had deem'd
Awake, that I had held a thought
Of parting, were with madness fraught;
I knew not woman's heart, alas!
Tho' lov'd, and loving-let it pass.-

**XIV**
I went from out the matted bow'r,
And hurried madly on my way;
And felt, with ev'ry flying hour,
That bore me from my home, more gay;
There isw of earth an agony
Which, ideal, still may be
The worst ill of mortality,
'Tis bliss, in its own reality,
Too real, to ***his*** breast who lives
Not within himself but gives
A portion of his willing soul
To God, and to the great whole-
To him, whose loving spirit will dwell
With Nature, in her wild paths; tell
Of her wond'rous ways, and telling bless
Her overpow'ring loveliness!
A more than agony to him
Whose failing sight will grow dim
With its own living gaze upon
That loveliness around: the sun-
The blue sky-the misty light
Of the pale blue cloud therein whose hue
Is grace to its heav'nly bed of blue;
Dim! tho' looking on all bright!
O God! when the thoughts that may not pass
Will burst upon him, and alas!
For the flight on Earth to Fancy giv'n,
There are no words-unless of Heav'n.

**XV**

Look 'round thee now on Samarcand,
Is she not queen of earth! her pride
Above all cities? in her hand
Their destinies? with all beside
Of glory, which the world hath known?
Stands she not proudly and alone?
And who her sov'reign? Timur he
Whom th' astonish'd earth hath seen,
With victory, on victory,
Redoubling age! and more, I ween.
The Zinghis' yet re-echoing fame,
And now what has he? what! a name.
The sound of revelry by night
Comes o'er me, with the mingled voice
Of many with a breast as light,
As if 'twere not the dying hour
Of one, in whom they did rejoice-
As in a leader,haply-Power
Its venom secretly imparts;
Nothing have I with human hearts.

**XVI**

When fortune mark'd me for her own,
And my proud hopes had reach'd a throne
(It boots me not, good friar , to tell
A tale the world but knows too well,
How by what hidden deeds of might,
I clamber'd to the tottering height,)
I still was young; and well I ween
My spirit what it e'er had been,
My eyes were still on pomp and power,
My wilde'd heart was far away,
In vallies of the wild Taglay,
In ine own Ada's matted bow'r,
I dwelt not long in Samarcand
Ere, in a peasant's lowly guise,
I sought my long-abandon'd land,
By sunset did its mountains rise
In dusky grandeur to my eyes:
But as I wander'd on the way
My heart sunk with the sun's ray,
To him, who still would gaze upon
The glory of the summer sun,
There comes, when that sun will from him part,
A sullen hopelessness of heart,

That soul will hate the ev'ning mist
So often lovely, and will lisp
To the sound of the coming darkness (known
To those whose spirits hark'n) as one
Who in a dream of night ***would*** fly
But cannot from a danger nigh,
What though the moon-the silvery moon
Shine on his path, in her high noon;
***Her*** smile is chilly, and ***her*** beam
In that time of dreariness will seem
As the portrait of one after death;
A likeness taken when the breath
Of young life, and the fire o' the eye
***Had*** lately been but had pass'd by.
'Tis thus when the lovely summer sun
Of our boyhood. his course has run:
For all we live to know-is known;
And all we seek to keep-hath flown;
With the noon-day beauty, which is all..
Let life, then as the day-flow'r fall-
The trancient, passionate day-flow'r,
Withering at the ev'ning hour.

**XVII**
I reached my home-my home no more-
For all was flown that made it so-
I pass'd from out its mossy door,
In vacant idlemess of woe.
There met me on its threshold stone;
A mountain hunter, I had known\
In childhood but he knew me not.
Something he spoke of the old cot:
It had seen better days, he said;
There rose a fountain once, and ***there***
Full many a fair flow'r rais'd its head:
But she who rear'd them was long dead,
And in such follies had no part,
What was there left me ***now***? despair-
A kingdom for a broken – heart.
then, as the day-flow'r, fall-
The trancient, passionate day-flow'r,
Withering at the ev'ning hour.

# WILLIAM WALKER

## May 8, 1824– September 12, 1860

William Walker was an American filibuster. He attempted to conquer several Latin American countries and appointed himself President of the Republic of Nicaragua in 1856 and ruled for only one year.. He was executed by the government of Honduras in 1860.

Born in Nashville, Tennessee, in 1824. His mother was Mary Norvell, the daughter of Lt. Lipscomb Norvell, a Revolutionary War officer who could trace his lineage back to the founding of Williamsburg. William Walker graduated ***summa cum laude*** from the University of Nashville at the ***early age of fourteen***. He traveled to Europe spending two years studying medicine at the universities of Edinburgh, Heidelberg, Göttingen, and Paris. The revolutions of 1848 took place during Walker's stay in Europe; the political influences he observed there were Garibaldi, Marx, Mazzini, Feuerbach, and Blanc, their fervour most possibly were influenced his filibustering aspirations.

At the age of 19, he received a medical degree from the University of Pennsylvania and practiced briefly in Philadelphia, then moved to New Orleans to study law. He soon left that profession to go into the publishing business and became co-owner and editor of the newspaper ***New Orleans Crescent*** in 1849.

Later he moved to San Francisco, California, and worked as a journalist. He also fought in three duels, in two of which he was wounded. Around that time, Walker probably from his first-hand experience of viewing the revoltionary spirit in Europe drew up his own plans and ideas to conquer areas in Latin America, with the object of creating states (and introduce slavery) ruled by white English speakers.

## His Expedition to Sonora

Walker traveled to Guaymas in 1853, and sought a grant from Mexico to create a colony to serve as bastion, a fortified frontier to protect the United States from Indians. Mexico declined his suggestion and he returned to San Francisco still determined to create the colony.

He began by recruiting American supporters of slavery, mainly inhabitants of Kentucky and Tennessee, and financed it by selling scripts which were redeemable in lands of Sonora, Mexico. He then decided to establish a Republic in Sonora, rather than a mere 'buffer zone'. He planned that if it should succeed he would incorporate the territory into the American Union of States. On October 15, 1853, Walker set out with 45 men on his first expedition: to conquer the Mexican territories Sonora and Baja. He captured La Paz and declared the new Republic of Baja California, with himself as president and his partner, Watkins, as vice president. He then decided to place the area under the laws of the American state of Louisiana, ***which made slavery legal***.

Afterwards he established his headquarters at Ensenada to maintain a more secure position and renamed the area. 'The the Republic of Sonora', in less than three months. Later, he incorporated Baja, California into part of the larger Republic of Snora.Lack of ordinance and supplies together with strong resistance by the Mexican government, forced Walker to relinquish his position, so he retreated. In California, he was put on trial for conducting an illegal war, (it violated American neutrality laws), expedition ***was popular in the southern*** and western United States. The jury took only eight minutes to acquit him.

# Conquest of Nicaragua

## First Battle of Rivas

A civil war was at that time in effect in the Central American republic of Nicaragua. To circumvent U.S. neutrality laws, Walker obtained a contract from President Castellón of the Nicaraguan Democratic Party to bring over three hundred "***colonists***" to Nicaragua.

The mercenaries received the right to bear arms in the service of the Democratic government. Walker sailed from San Francisco on May 3, 1855, with approximately 60 men. Upon landing, the force was reinforced by 170 locals and about 100 Americans, including the well-known explorer and journalist Charles Wilkins Webber and the English adventurer Charles Frederick Henningsen, a veteran of the First Carlist War, The Hungarian Revolution, and the war in Circassia.

A reporter from the ***Sacramento Union***, Albert Jennings Fountain, went to Nicaragua to cover Walker's adventures there. When he sent back reports that Walker was attempting to set up a slave-holding republic in Nicaragua, Walker ***sentenced him to death by a firing squad***. He eventually ***escaped disguised as a woman***.

Walker's agents recruited American and European men to sail to the region and fight for the conquest of the other four Central American nations: Guatemala, El Salvador, Honduras, and Costa Rica.He recruited over a thousand American and European mercenaries, many of whom were transported free by the 'Cornelius Vanderbilt's Accessory Transit Company.' This eventually failed when an outraged Vanderbilt led a coalition to stop money and supplies from reaching Walker.

At the time, a major trade route between New York City and San Francisco ran through southern Nicaragua. Ships from New York would enter the San Juan River from the Atlantic and sail across Lake Nicaragua. People and goods would then be transported by stagecoach over a narrow strip of land near the city of Rivas, before reaching the Pacific and being shipped to San Francisco.The commercial exploitation of this route had been granted by a former Nicaraguan administration to the Accessory Transit Company. With Castellón's consent, Walker attacked the Legitimists in the town of Rivas, near the trans-isthmian route. He was driven off, but not without inflicting heavy casualties.

On September 4, during the Battle of La Virgen, Walker defeated the Nicaraguan national army. On October 13, he conquered the capital of Granada and took effective control of the country. Initially, as commander of the army, Walker ruled Nicaragua through puppet President Patricio Rivas. U.S. President Franklin Pierce recognized Walker's regime as the legitimate governor of Nicaragua on May 20, 1856.

When Walker arrived in Nicaragua, C.K. Garrison and Charles Morgan, subordinates of Cornelius Vanderbilt's Accessory Transit Company, offered financial assistance with Walker's expedition ***in a plot to seize control of Vanderbilt's company***. In return, Walker seized the company's property on the pretext of a charter violation and turned the company over to Garrison and Morgan. Vanderbilt then spread rumors that the company was issuing stock illegally in order to depress its value, allowing him to regain controlling interest. As ruler of Nicaragua, Walker then revoked the Transit Company's charter, claiming that it had violated the agreement, and granted use of the route back to Garrison and Morgan.

Outraged, Vanderbilt successfully pressured the U.S. government to withdraw its recognition of Walker's regime. Walker had also scared his neighbors and American and European investors with talk of ***further military conquests in Central America***. Juan Rafael Mora, President of Costa Rica, became aware of Walker's intentions and declared war on him.

Walker sent Colonel Schlessinger to invade Costa Rica in a preemptive action, but his forces were defeated at the Battle of Santa Rosa in March 1856. Vanderbilt financed and trained a military coalition of these states, led by Costa Rica, and worked to prevent men and supplies from reaching Walker. He also provided defectors from Walker's army with payments and free passage back to the U.S. In April 1856, Costa Rican troops and American mercenaries supported by Vanderbilt penetrated into Nicaraguan territory and inflicted a defeat on Walker's men at the Second Battle of Rivas, in which Juan Santamaría, later to be recognized as one of Costa Rica's national heroes, played a key role.

## Walker as President of Nicaragua

Walker set himself up as ***President of Nicaragua***, after conducting a farcical election and was inaugurated on July 12, 1856 He then launched an Americanization program and declared English as the official language and reorganized the currency and fiscal policy to encourage immigration from the United States.

Realizing that his position was becoming precarious, ***he sought support from the Southerners in the U.S***. by recasting his campaign as a fight ***to spread the institution of black slavery***, which many American Southern businessmen saw as the basis of their agrarian economy. With this in mind, Walker revoked Nicaragua's emancipation edict of 1824. This move did increase Walker's popularity in the South and attracted the attention of Pierre Soulé, an influential New Orleans politician, who campaigned to raise support for Walker's war. Nevertheless, Walker's army, weakened by an epidemic of cholera and massive defections, was no match for the Central American coalition and Vanderbilt's agents.

## Returned by the U.S. Navy

On May 1, 1857, ***Walker surrendered to Commander Charles Henry Davis*** of the United States Navy and was repatriated. Upon disembarking in New York City, he was greeted as a hero, but he alienated public opinion when he blamed his defeat on the U.S. Navy. ***Within six months, he set off on another expedition***, but he was arrested by the U.S. Navy Home Squadron under the command of Commodore Hiram Paulding and once again returned to the U.S. amid considerable public controversy over the legality of the Navy's actions.

## Death in Honduras

After writing an account of his Central American campaign (published in 1860 as ***War in Nicaragua***), Walker once again returned to the region.The British government was trying to reduce its holdings in the region so it was giving established governments in central America its land possessions in the continent. British colonists on the Island of Roatan, which was owned by Honduras. Knowing of Walker's reputation they approached him to help establish a separate government there. He disembarked in the port city of Trujillo, in the Republic of Honduras, but soon ***fell into the custody of Captain Salmon of the British Royal Navy***.

The British government ***controlled the neighboring regions of British Honduras (now Belize) and the Mosquito Coast*** (now part of Nicaragua) and had considerable strategic and economic interest in the construction of an inter-oceanic canal through Central America. It therefore regarded Walker as a menace to its own affairs in the region.
Rather than return him to the U.S., Capt. Salmon delivered Walker to the Honduran authorities, who ***executed him*** near the site of the present-day hospital by firing squad on September 12, 1860. Walker was 36 years old.

***He is buried in the Cementerio Viejo in the coastal town of Trujillo, Colón.***

## Influence and Reputation

William Walker convinced many Southerners of the desirability of creating a slave-holding empire in tropical Latin America. In 1861, when U.S. Senator John J. Crittenden proposed that the 36°30' parallel north be declared as a line of demarcation between free and slave territories,.

Some Republicans denounced such an arrangement, saying that it "would amount to a perpetual covenant of war against every people, tribe, and State owning a foot of land between here and Tierra del Fuego."

Before the end of the American Civil War, Walker's memory enjoyed great popularity in the southern and western United States, where he was known as "General Walker" and as the "grey-eyed man of destiny." Northerners, on the other hand, generally regarded him as a pirate. Despite his intelligence and personal charm, Walker consistently proved to be a limited military and political leader. Unlike men of similar ambition, such as Cecil Rhodes, Walker's grandiose scheming ultimately failed.

In Central American countries, the successful military campaign of 1856-1857 against William Walker became a source of national pride and identity, and it was later promoted by local historians and politicians as substitute for the war of independence that Central America had not experienced. April 11 is a Costa Rican national holiday in memory of Walker's defeat at Rivas. Juan Santamaría, who played a key role in that battle, is honored as the Costa Rican national hero.

Although Walker is far better known today in Central America than he is the United States, he does have a number of interesting ties to Nashville, Tennessee, the city of his birth. Locally, Walker is remembered as the only native Nashvillian ever to become a head of state, and a historical marker commemorates his birthplace, downtown not far from Second Avenue.

William Walker wrote his own account of his involvement in Nicaragua. A facsimile copy of the Title Page is shown below and his Preface.

# WAR IN NICARAGUA

WRITTEN BY

GEN'L WILLIAM WALKER

**MOBILE;**

**S.H.GOETZEL & CO.**

**NEW- YORK ; 82 WARREN ST.**

Entered according to an Act of Congress in the year 1860 -
by S.H. GOETZEL & Co.
In the Clerk's office of the District Court of the United States for the Southern District of New- York

I dedicate this effort to do justice to their acts and motives: To the living, with the hope that we may soon meet again on the soil for which we have suffered more than the pangs of death-the reproaches of a people for whose welfare we stood ready to die: To the memory of those who perished in the struggle, with the vow that as long as life lasts no peace shall remain with the foes who libel their names and strive to tear away the laurel which hangs over their graves.
W .W.

## PREFACE

No history is so hard to write as that of our own times. Few, if any, can free themselves from the fashions of thought and opinion which control the daily life of their neighbors, and every one inhales to some extent the vapors floating in the air he hourly breathes. The task is even more difficult if a man attempts to narrate events in which he has taken part.

As the soldier, warmed by the heat of battle, dimly sees through the dust and smoke of a well-fought field, the large movements which decide the issue of the conflict, so he who has mingled in the struggles of parties or the contests of nations, may not be as well fitted as others to speak of facts moulded partially by his own will and hand. But if the memoir writer be fair and discreet, he may contribute materials for future use, and his very errors may instruct after ages.

The author of the following narrative does not expect to attain perfect truth in all things; he merely asks the reader to give him credit for the desire to state facts accurately, and to reason justly about the circumstances attending the presence of the Americans in Nicaragua

***March 1st. 1860***

# PHOEBE CARY

Phoebe Cary was an American poet, the younger sister of poet Alice Cary (1820–1871). The sisters co-published poems in 1849, and then each went on to publish volumes of her own. After their deaths in 1871, joint anthologies of the sisters' unpublished poems were compiled.

Phoebe was born, September 4, 1824, at Mount Healthy, Ohio near Cincinnati, they both were raised on the Clovernook farm in North College Hill, Ohio in a Universalist household, they held liberal and reformist religious and political views, and also attended Methodist, Presbyterian, and Congregationalist services and were amiable with ministers of all these denominationsThey occasionally attended school but the sisters were often needed to work at home and so became mainly self-educated. Phoebe was more outgoing than her sister, she became ***a champion of women's*** **rights** and for a short time edited ***The Revolution***, a newspaper published by Susan B. Anthony.

In 1848, their poetry was published in the anthology ***Female Poets of America*** edited by Rufus Wilmot Griswold and, with his help, ***Poems of Alice and Phoebe Cary*** was published in 1849. Poet John Greenleaf Whittier had been invited to provide a preface but refused. He believed their poetry did not need his endorsement and also noted a general dislike for prefaces as a method to "pass off by aid of a known name, what otherwise would not pass current".

The sisters' anthology garnered much acclaim, and in 1850 they moved to New York City. There, they often hosted evening receptions on Sundays, some of which were attended by well-known figures such as P. T. Barnum, John Greenleaf Whittier, and Elizabeth Cady Stanton.

While in New York, Phoebe published two volumes of exclusively her own poetry: ***Poems and Parodies*** and ***Poems of Faith, Hope, and Love***. Additionally, her lyrics appeared in many church hymnals, on Sunday School cards, and in household scrapbooks.

One of her hymns, "Nearer Home," was often sung at funerals, including Alice's and her own.Alice died in 1871 from tuberculosis; Phoebe died five months later of hepatitison July 31, 1871, in Newport, Rhode Island. Her burial was in Green-Wood Cemetery, Brooklyn, New York.

***SUPPOSE***
by Phoebe Cary

Suppose little lady,
Your doll should break her head,
Could you make it whole by crying
Till your eyes and nose are red?
And wouldn't it be pleasanter
To treat is as a joke;

And say you're glad "'Twas Dolly's
And not your head that broke?"
Suppose you're dressed for walking,
And the rain comes pouring down,
Will it clear off any sooner
Because you scold and frown?

And wouldn't it be nicer
For you to smile than pout,
And so make sunshine in the house
When there is none without?
Suppose your task, my little man,
Is very hard to get,
Will it make it easier
For you to sit and fret?

And wouldn't it be wiser
Than waiting like a dunce,
To go to work in earnest,
And learn the thing at once?
Suppose that some boys had a horse,
And some a coach and pair,
Will it tire you less by walking
To say, "It is n't fair?"

And would n't it be nobler
To keep your temper sweet,
And in your heart be thankful
You can walk upon your feet?
And suppose the world don't please you,
Nor the way some people do,
Do you think the whole creation
Will be altered just for you?

And is n't it, my boy or girl,
The wisest, bravest plan,
Whatever comes, or doesn't come,
To do the best you can?

# ALICE CARY

**April 26, 1820 – February 12, 1871**

Alice Cary was born on April 26, 1820, in Mount Healthy, Ohio near Cincinnati. Her parents lived on a farm bought by Robert Cary in 1813 in what is now North College Hill, Ohio. He called the 27 acres Clovernook Farm. The farm was 10 miles north of Cincinnati, a good distance from schools, and the father could not afford to give their large family of nine children a very good education. But Alice and her sister Phoebe were fond of reading and studied all they could. They became self-educated.

While the sisters were raised in a Universalist household and held political and religious views that were liberal and reformist, they often attended Methodist, Presbyterian, and Congregationalist services and were amiable with ministers of all these denominations and others. According to Phoebe.

Whilst liberal and unsectarian in her views, [Alice] always preserved kept an attachment her parents church accepting its doctrines. She was a firm believer of christian brotherhood and in God's kindness where she believed that even the worst sinner will be accepted by the 'Father' who will add him to the flock and give him compassion.

When Alice was 17 and Phoebe 13, they began to write verses, which were printed in newspapers. Alice's first major poem, "The Child of Sorrow," was published in 1838 and was praised by influential critics including Edgar Allan Poe, Rufus Wilmot Griswold, and Horace Greeley.

The anthology made Alice and Phoebe well-known, and in 1850 they moved to New York City, where they devoted themselves to writing, and garnered much fame. There, they also hosted receptions on Sunday evenings attended by such notables as P. T. Barnum, Elizabeth Cady Stanton, and John Greenleaf Whittier. In addition to poetry, Alice wrote several stories in prose, among which were ***The Clovernook Children*** and ***Snow Berries, a Book for Young Folks***. She died of tuberculosis in 1871 in New York at age 51. The pallbearers at her funeral included P. T. Barnum and Horace Greeley. Alice Cary is buried alongside her sister Phoebe in Green-Wood Cemetery, Brooklyn

### *A DREAM*

I dreamed I had a plot of ground,
Once when I chanced asleep to drop,
And that a green hedge fenced it round,
Cloudy with roses at the top.

I saw a hundred mornings rise,
So far a little dream may reach,
And Spring with Summer in her eyes
Making the chiefest charm of each.

A thousand vines were climbing o'er
The hedge, I thought, but as I tried
To pull them down, for evermore
The flowers dropt off the other side!

Waking, I said, "These things are signs
Sent to insruct us that 'tis ours
Duly to keep and dress our vines,
Waiting in patience for the flowers.

"And when the angel feared of all
Across my hearth its shadow spread,
The rose that climbed my garden wall
Has bloomed the other side," I said.

—Alice Cary

### *AUTUMN*

Shorter and shorter now the twilight clips
The days, as through the sunset gates they crowd,
And Summer from her golden collar slips
And strays through stubble-fields, and moans aloud,

Save when by fits the warmer air deceives,
And, stealing hopeful to some sheltered bower,
She lies on pillows of the yellow leaves,
And tries the old tunes over for an hour.

The wind, whose tender whisper in the May
Set all the young blooms listening through th'grove,
Sits rustling in the faded boughs to-day
And makes his cold and unsuccessful love.

The rose has taken off her tire of red—
The mullein-stalk its yellow stars have lost,
And the proud meadow-pink hangs down her head
Against erth's chilly bosom, witched with frost.

The robin, that was busy all the June,
Before the sun had kissed the topmost bough,
Catching our hearts up in his golden tune,
Has given place to the brown cricket now.

The very cock crows lonesomely at morn—
Each flag and fern the shrinking stream divides—
Uneasy cattle low, and lambs forlorn
Creep to their strawy sheds with nettled sides.

Shut up the door: who loves me must not look
Upon the withered world, but haste to bring
His lighted candle, and his story-book,
And live with me the poetry of Spring

—Alice Cary

# JAMES BOWIE

**April 10, 1796 – March 6, 1836**

Kentucky born; Jim Bowie a 19th-century American pioneer and soldier spent most of his life in Louisiana, where he was raised and later worked as a land speculator. His rise to fame began in 1827 on reports of the Sandbar Fight. What began as a duel between two other men deteriorated into a melee in which Bowie, having been shot and stabbed, killed the sheriff of Rapides Parish with a large knife. This, and other stories of Bowie's prowess with the knife, led to the widespread popularity of the Bowie knife. He played a prominent role in the Texas Revolution, culminating in his death at the Battle of the Alamo.

Countless stories of him as a fighter and frontiersman, both real and fictitious, have made him a legendary figure in Texas history and a folk hero of American culture.Bowie's reputation was cemented by his role in the Texas Revolution. After moving to Texas in 1830, Bowie became a Mexican citizen and married the daughter of the vice governor of the province. His fame in Texas grew following his failed expedition to find the lost San Saba mine, during which his small party repelled an attack by a large Indian raiding party.

At the outbreak of the Texas Revolution, Bowie joined the Texas militia, leading forces at the Battle of Concepción and the Grass Fight. In January 1836, he arrived at the Alamo, where he commanded the volunteer forces until an illness left him bedridden. Bowie died with the other Alamo defenders on March 6. Despite conflicting accounts of the manner of his death, the "most popular, and probably the most accurate" accounts maintain that he died in his bed after emptying his pistols into several Mexican soldiers.

According to his older brother, John, James Bowie was born in Logan County, Kentucky, in the spring of 1796 Historian Raymond Thorp gave his birth date as April 10, but Thorp did not provide any documentation for that date Bowie was the ninth of ten children born to Elve Ap-Catesby Jones and Rezin Bowie.

His father had been injured while fighting in the American Revolution, and in 1782 married the young woman who had nursed him back to health. The Bowies moved frequently, first settling in Georgia, before moving to Kentucky. At the time of Bowie's birth, his father owned eight slaves, eleven head of cattle, seven horses, and one stud horse. The following year the family acquired 200 acres (80 ha) along the Red River. They sold that property in 1800 and relocated to Missouri before moving to Spanish Louisiana in 1802, where they settled on Bushley Bayou in Rapides Parish.

The Bowie family moved again in 1809, settling on Bayou Teche in Louisiana before finding a permanent home in Opelousas in 1812. The Bowie children were raised on the frontier and even as small children were expected to help clear the land and plant crops. All of the Bowie children learned to read and write in English, but Jim and his elder brother Rezin could also read, write, and speak Spanish and French fluently. The children learned to survive on the frontier, how to fish and run a farm and plantation. Jim Bowie became proficient with pistol, rifle, and knife, and had a reputation for fearlessness. As a boy one of his Indian friends even taught him to rope alligators.

In response to Andrew Jackson's plea for volunteers to fight the British in the War of 1812, Bowie and his brother Rezin enlisted in the Louisiana militia in late 1814. The war ended on December 24 of that year with the signing of the Treaty of Ghent, and the Bowie brothers arrived in New Orleans too late to participate in the fighting. After mustering out of the militia, Bowie settled in Rapides Parish, where he supported himself by sawing planks and lumber and floating it down the bayou for sale. In June 1819, he joined the Long expedition, an effort to liberate Texas from Spanish rule. The group encountered little resistance and, after capturing Nacogdoches, declared Texas an independent republic. The extent of Bowie's participation is unclear, but he returned to Louisiana before the invasion was repelled by Spanish troops.

Shortly before their father died in 1818 or 1819, he gave ten slaves, and horses and cattle to both Jim and his brother Rezin. For the next seven years the brothers worked together to develop several large estates in Lafourche Parish and Opelousas Louisiana's population was growing rapidly, and the brothers hoped to take advantage of its rising land prices through speculation. Without the capital required to buy large tracts, they entered into a partnership with a pirate, Jean Lafitte, in 1818 to raise money. By then, the United States had outlawed the importation of slaves, and most southern states allowed anyone who informed on a slave trader to receive half of what the imported slaves would earn at auction as a reward. Bowie made three trips to Lafitte's compound on Galveston Island. On each occasion he bought smuggled slaves and then took them directly to a customhouse to inform on his own actions. When the customs officers offered the slaves for auction, Bowie purchased them and received back half the price he had paid, as allowed by the state laws. He then could legally transport the slaves and resell them at a greater market value in New Orleans or areas farther up the Mississippi River. Using this scheme the brothers collected $65,000 to be used for their land speculation.

In 1825, the two brothers joined with their younger brother Stephen to buy Acadia, a plantation near Alexandria. Within two years they had established the first steam mill in Louisiana to be used for grinding sugar cane. The plantation became known as a model estate, but, on February 12, 1831, they sold it and 65 slaves for $90,000. With their profits, Bowie and Rezin bought a plantation in Arkansas. Bowie and his brother John were involved in a major court case in the late 1820s over their land speculation.

When the United States purchased the Louisiana Territory in 1803, it promised to honor all former land grant claims, and for the next 20 years efforts were made to establish who owned what land. In May 1824, Congress authorized the superior courts of each territory to hear suits from people who claimed they had been overlooked. The Arkansas Superior Court received 126 claims in late 1827 from residents who claimed to have purchased land in former Spanish grants from the Bowie brothers. Although the Superior Court originally confirmed most of those claims, the decisions were reversed in February 1831, after further research showed that the land had never belonged to the Bowies, and that the original land grant documentation had been forged. The U.S. Supreme Court upheld the reversal in 1833. When the disgruntled purchasers considered suing the Bowies, they discovered that the documents in the case had been removed from the court; left without evidence, they declined to pursue a case

Bowie became internationally famous as a result of a feud with Norris Wright, the sheriff of Rapides Parish. Bowie had supported Wright's opponent in the race for sheriff, and Wright, a bank director, had been instrumental in turning down Bowie's loan application. After a confrontation in Alexandria one afternoon, Wright fired a shot at Bowie. The uninjured Bowie was enraged and tried to kill Wright with his bare hands. Wright's friends intervened and stopped the attack, after which Bowie resolved to carry his hunting knife at all times. The knife he carried had a huge blade that was 9.25 inches (23.5 cm) long and 1.5 inches (3.8 cm) wide.

The following year, on September 19, 1827, Bowie and Wright attended a duel on a sandbar outside of Natchez, Mississippi. Bowie supported duelist Samuel Levi Wells III, while Wright supported Wells's opponent, Dr. Thomas Harris Maddox. The duelists each fired two shots, and, as neither man had been injured, resolved their duel with a handshake.

Other members of the groups, who had various reasons for disliking each other, began fighting. Bowie was shot in the hip; after regaining his feet he drew a knife, described as a butcher knife, and charged his attacker. The attacker hit Bowie over the head with his empty pistol, breaking the pistol and knocking Bowie to the ground. Wright shot at and missed the prone Bowie, who returned fire and possibly, hit Wright. Wright then drew his sword cane and impaled Bowie. When Wright attempted to retrieve his blade by placing his foot on Bowie's chest and tugging, Bowie pulled him down and disemboweled Wright with his large knife. Wright died instantly, and Bowie, with Wright's sword still protruding from his chest, was shot again and stabbed by another member of the group. The doctors who had been present for the duel retrieved the bullets and patched Bowie's other wounds.

Newspapers picked up the story, which became known as the Sandbar Fight, and described in detail Bowie's fighting prowess and his unusual knife. Witness accounts agreed that Bowie did not attack first, and the others had focused their attack on Bowie because "they considered him the most dangerous man among their opposition." The fight cemented Bowie's reputation across the South as a superb knife-fighter.

There is disagreement among scholars as to whether the knife used in this fight was the same kind of knife now known as a Bowie knife. Multiple accounts exist of who designed and built the first Bowie knife. Some claim that Bowie designed it, while others attribute the design to noted knife makers of the time. However, in a letter to ***The Planter's Advocate*, *Rezin Bowie claimed to have invented the knife*,** and many Bowie family members as well as "most authorities on the Bowie knife tend to believe it was invented by" Rezin Rezin Bowie's grandchildren, however, claimed that Rezin merely supervised his blacksmith, who was the creator of the knife.

After the Sandbar Fight and subsequent battles in which Bowie successfully used his knife to defend himself, the Bowie knife became very popular. Many craftsmen and manufacturers made their own versions, and major cities of the Southwest had "Bowie knife schools", which taught "the art of cut, thrust, and parry." His fame, and that of his knife, spread to England, and by the early 1830s many British manufacturers were producing Bowie knives for shipment to the United States. The design of the knife continued to evolve, but today a Bowie knife generally is considered to have a blade 8.25 inches (21.0 cm) long and 1.25 inches (3.2 cm) wide, with a curved point, a "sharp false edge cut from both sides", and a cross-guard to protect the user's hands.

After recovering from the wounds he suffered in the Sandbar Fight, in 1828 Bowie decided to move to Texas, at that time a state in the Mexican federation The 1824 Constitution of Mexico banned religions other than Roman Catholicism and gave preference to Mexican citizens in receiving land Bowie was baptized into the Roman Catholic faith in San Antonio on April 28, 1828, sponsored by the alcalde (chief administrator) of the town, Juan Martin de Veramendi and the wife of the administrator, Josefa Navarro.

For the next eighteen months Bowie travelled through Louisiana and Mississippi. In 1829, he became engaged to Cecilia Wells, who died in Alexandria on September 29, two weeks before their wedding.

On January 1, 1830, Bowie left Louisiana for permanent residency in Texas. He stopped at Nacogdoches, at Jared E. Groce's farm on the Brazos River, and in San Felipe, where Bowie presented a letter of introduction to Stephen F. Austin from Thomas F. McKinney, one of the Old Three Hundred colonists. On February 20, Bowie took an oath of allegiance to Mexico and then proceeded to San Antonio de Bexar. At the time the city, known as Bexar, had a population of 2,500 people, mostly of Mexican descent, and Bowie's fluency in Spanish helped him establish himself in the area. Bowie was elected a commander of the Texas Rangers later that year. Although the Rangers would not be organized officially until 1835, Stephen F. Austin had founded the group by employing thirty men to keep the peace and protect the colonists from attacks by hostile Indians. Other areas assembled similar volunteer militias, and Bowie commanded a group of the volunteers

Bowie ***became a Mexican citizen*** on September 30, 1830, after promising to establish textile mills in the province of Coahuila y Tejas. To fulfill his promise, Bowie entered into partnership with Veramendi to build cotton and wool mills in Saltillo.

With his citizenship assured, Bowie now had the right to buy up to 11 leagues of public land. He convinced fourteen or fifteen other citizens to apply for land in order to turn it over to him, giving him 700,000 acres (280,000 ha) for speculation. Bowie may have been the first to induce settlers to apply for empresario grants which could then be sold in bulk to speculators like Bowie. The Mexican government passed laws in 1834 and 1835 that stopped much of the land speculation. On April 25, 1831 Bowie married 19-year-old Maria Ursula de Veramendi, the daughter of his business partner, who had become the vice-governor of the province. At the time Bowie claimed to have a net worth of $223,000, mostly in land of questionable title. Bowie also lied ***about his age, claiming to be 30 rather than 35***. The couple built a house in San Antonio, on land Veramendi had given them near the San José Mission. They decided however, to move into the Veramendi Palace, and lived with Ursula's parents, who supplied them with spending money. The couple had two children, Marie Elve, born March 20, 1832, and James Veramendi, born July 18, 1833.

Shortly after his marriage Bowie became fascinated with the story of the "lost" Los Almagres Mine[1], said to be west of San Antonio near the ruin of Santa Cruz de San Sabá Mission. The mine had been operated by local Indians before being seized by the Spanish. After Mexico won independence from Spain, government interest in the mines waned. A number of hostile Indian tribes roamed the area, including Comanche, Lipan Apache, and Karankawa, and without government troops to keep the tribes at bay, mining ceased. It was believed that after the Mexican citizens left the area, the Lipan Apaches took over the mines.

Bowie obtained permission from the Mexican government and mounted an expedition into Indian territory to search for the legendary silver mine, Bowie, his brother Rezin, and nine others set out for San Saba on November 2, 1831. Six miles (10 km) from their goal, the group stopped to negotiate with a large Indian raiding party following them. The attempts at parley failed and Bowie and his group fought for their lives for the next 13 hours. When the Indians finally retreated, Bowie reportedly had lost only one man, while over 40 Indians had been killed and 30 more wounded. In the meantime, a party of friendly Comanche Indians rode into San Antonio, bringing word of the raiding party, which outnumbered the Bowie expedition by 15–to–1

The citizens of San Antonio believed the Bowie expedition must have perished, and Ursula Bowie began wearing widow's weeds. However, the surviving members of the group returned to San Antonio on December 6. Bowie's report of the expedition, written in Spanish, printed in several newspapers, further establishing his reputation. He set out again with a larger force the following month, but returned home empty-handed after two and a half months of searching.

---

1 "Silver! Enough for every person to own a silver mine! wrote Bernardo de Miranda y Flores in his 1756 report to the Spanish provincial governor after visiting Cerro del Almagre and Los Almagres, a mine near the Llano River. Almagre is a Spanish word that means "ochre", and Cerro del Almagre means a Mountain of Ochre. . In 1753, a small group of Spaniards excavated a pit at the. Later, the governor asked Miranda to visit and examine the site. Miranda cleared the pit, extracted samples, and had them assayed. Although the results showed little silver, Miranda was convinced that silver-bearing ore could be extracted in large quantities because of the extent of iron oxide rock he observed. Unfortunately for the Spaniards, this land was occupied by Apaches who killed prospectors in the area during the next few years.***Source; Caran, S. Christopher - 2000 The Lost Spanish Silver Mines of Llano County, Texas. Texas Heritage 18 (4)l:9- 35, Texas Historical Foundation, Austin.***

Bowie never talked of his exploits despite his increasing fame. Captain William Y. Lacey, who spent eight months living in the wilderness with Bowie, described him as a humble man who never used profanity or vulgarities.

Between 1830 and 1832 the Mexican Congress passed a series of laws that seemed to discriminate against Anglo colonists in the province of Coahuila y Tejas, increasing tension between the Anglo citizenry and Mexican officials. In response to the rumblings, Mexican troops established military posts in several locations within the province, including San Antonio de Béxar Although much of the military supported the administration of President Anastasio Bustamante, Antonio López de Santa Anna led an insurrection against him in 1832. Anglo colonists in Texas supported Santa Anna and General José Antonio Mexía, who led soldiers into Texas to oust commanders loyal to Bustamante

After hearing that the Mexican army commander in Nacogdoches, José de las Piedras, had demanded that all residents in his area surrender their arms, Bowie cut short a visit to Natchez in July 1832 to return to Texas. On August 2, 1832, he joined a group of other Texians and marched into Nacogdoches to "present their demands" to Piedras. Before the group reached the building housing the town officials, they were attacked by a force of 100 Mexican cavalry.

The Texians returned fire and, after the cavalry retreated, initiated a siege of the garrison. After a second battle in which Piedras lost 33 men, the Mexican army evacuated during the night. Bowie and eighteen companions ambushed the fleeing army and, after Piedras fled, marched the soldiers back to Nacogdoches Bowie later served as a delegate to the Convention of 1833, which formally requested that Texas become its own state within the Mexican federation.

Several months later, a cholera epidemic struck Texas. Fearing the disease would reach San Antonio, Bowie sent his pregnant wife and their daughter to the family estate in Monclova in the company of her parents and brother. The cholera epidemic ***instead struck Monclova***, and between September 6 and September 14, Ursula, their children, her brother, and her parents all died of the disease. Bowie, on business in Natchez, heard of his family's deaths in November. From then on, he drank heavily and became "careless in his dress".

The following year the Mexican government passed new laws allowing land sale in Texas, and Bowie returned to land speculation. He was appointed as a land commissioner, tasked with promoting settlement in the area purchased by John T. Mason. His appointment ended in May 1835, when President Antonio López de Santa Anna abolished the Coahuila y Tejas government and ordered the arrest of all Texians (including Bowie) doing business in Monclova. Bowie was forced to flee Monclova and return to the Anglo areas of Texas.

The Anglos in Texas began agitating for war against Santa Anna, and Bowie worked with William B. Travis, the leader of the War Party, to gain support. Bowie visited several Indian villages in East Texas in an attempt to convince the reluctant tribes to fight against the Mexican government. Santa Anna responded to the rumblings by ordering large numbers of Mexican troops to Texas.

The Texas Revolution began on October 2, 1835 with the Battle of Gonzales. Stephen F. Austin formed an army of 500 men to march on the Mexican forces in San Antonio with the cannon that had precipitated the fight. On October 22, Austin asked Bowie, now a colonel in the volunteer militia, and James W. Fannin to scout the area around the missions of San Francisco de la Espada and San José y San Miguel de Aguayo to find supplies for the volunteer forces. The scouting party left with 92 men, many of them members of the New Orleans Grays who had just arrived in Texas. After discovering a good defensive position near Mission Concepción, the group requested that Austin's army join them.

On the foggy morning of October 28, Mexican General Domingo Ugartechea led a force of 300 infantry and cavalry soldiers and 2 small cannons against the Texian forces Although the Mexican army was able to get within 200 yards (183 m), the Texian defensive position protected them from fire. As the Mexicans stopped to reload their cannon, the Texians climbed a bluff and picked off some of the soldiers. The stalemate ended shortly after ***Bowie led a charge to seize one of the Mexican cannons***, at that time only 80 yards (73 m) away. Ugartechea retreated with his troops, ending the Battle of Concepción. One Texian and ten Mexican troops had been killed One of the men under Bowie's command during the battle later praised him "as a born leader, never needlessly spending a bullet or imperiling a life, who repeatedly admonished "***Keep under cover boys, and reserve your fire; we haven't a man to spare***."

An hour after the battle ended, Austin arrived with the rest of the Texian army to begin a siege of San Antonio de Béxar, where General Martín Perfecto de Cós, the overall commander of Mexican forces in Texas, and his troops were garrisoned. Two days later, Bowie resigned from Austin's army because he did not have an official commission in the army, and he disliked the "minor tasks of scouting and spying"

On November 3, 1835, Texas declared itself an independent state, and a provisional government was formed with Henry Smith of Brazoria elected provisional governor. Austin requested to be relieved of his command of the army, and Sam Houston was named army chief. Edward Burleson was chosen as temporary commander of the troops in San Antonio. Bowie appeared before the council at some point and spoke for an hour, asking for a commission. The council refused Bowie's request, likely because of lingering animosity over his land dealings.

Houston offered Bowie a commission as an officer on his staff, but Bowie rejected the opportunity, explaining that he wanted to be in the midst of the fighting. Instead, Bowie enlisted in the army as a private under Fannin. He distinguished himself again in the Grass Fight on November 26. Cós had sent 100 soldiers to cut grass for the horses.

As they returned to San Antonio, Bowie took 60 mounted men to intercept the party, which they believed carried valuable cargo The Mexican troops quickened their pace in the hopes of reaching the safety of the city, but Bowie and his cavalry chased them. At the end of the fight, the Texians had two wounded men, but had captured many horses and mules.

Shortly after Bowie left San Antonio, Ben Milam led an assault on the city. In the ensuing fighting, the Texians suffered only a few casualties, while the Mexican army lost many troops to death and desertion. Cós surrendered and returned to Mexico, taking with him the last Mexican troops in Texas. Believing the war was over, many of the Texian volunteers left the army and returned to their families. In early January 1836, Bowie went to San Felipe and asked the council to allow him to recruit a regiment. He again was turned down, as he "was not an officer of the government nor army."

After Houston received word that Santa Anna was leading a large force to San Antonio, Bowie offered to lead volunteers to defend the Alamo from the expected attack. He arrived with 30 men on January 19 where they found a force of 104 men with a few weapons and a few cannons, but little supplies and gunpowder. Houston knew that there were not enough men to hold the fort in an attack and had given Bowie orders to remove the artillery and blow up the fortification. Bowie and the Alamo captain, James C. Neill, decided they did not have enough oxen to move the artillery, and they did not want to destroy the fortress. On January 26, one of Bowie's men, James Bonham, organized a rally which passed a resolution in favor of holding the Alamo. Bonham signed the resolution first, with Bowie's signature second.

Through Bowie's connections because of his marriage and his fluency in Spanish, the predominantly Mexican population of San Antonio often furnished him with information about the movements of the Mexican army. After learning that Santa Anna had 4,500 troops and was heading for the city,

Bowie wrote several letters to the provisional government asking for help in defending the Alamo, especially "men, money, rifles, and cannon powder". In another letter, to Governor Smith, he reiterated his view that "the salvation of Texas depends in great measure on keeping Bexar out of the hands of the enemy. It serves as the frontier picquet guard, and if it were in the possession of Santa Anna, there is no stronghold from which to repel him in his march toward the Sabine." The letter to Smith ended, "Colonel Neill and myself have come to the solemn resolution that we will rather die in these ditches than give it up to the enemy."

On February 3, William Travis arrived with an additional 30 troops, and several days later Davy Crockett appeared with twelve Tennesseans. Neill went on furlough on February 17 to visit his sick family, leaving Travis, a member of the regular army, in command Bowie was older than Travis with a better reputation and considered himself a colonel, thus outranking Travis, a major He refused to answer to Travis, who called an election for the men to choose their own commander. They chose Bowie, infuriating Travis Bowie celebrated his appointment by getting very drunk and causing havoc in San Antonio, releasing all prisoners in the local jails and harassing citizens. Travis was disgusted, but two days later the men agreed to a joint command; Bowie would command the volunteers, and Travis would command the regular army and the volunteer cavalry.

Fearing for the safety of his wife's relatives in San Antonio, Bowie invited her cousins Getrudis Navarro and Juana Navarro Alsbury, as well as Alsbury's 18-month-old son, Alijo, to stay inside the walls of the Alamo. Bowie had been ill, and two doctors, including the fort surgeon, were unable to diagnose his illness. Travis became the sole commander of the forces when Bowie was confined to bed. Santa Anna and his army reached the outskirts of San Antonio de Bexar several days later and began a siege of the Alamo on February 24. The Mexican army raised a red flag to warn the defenders that no quarter would be given

Travis sent Juan Seguin to recruit reinforcements on February 25, and 32 additional men arrived. Thirty-five years after the Alamo fell, a reporter identified Louis "Moses" Rose as the only man to have "deserted" the Texian forces at the Alamo. According to the reporter's version of Rose's account, when Travis realized that the Mexican army would likely prevail, he drew a line in the sand and asked those willing to die for the cause to cross the line. At Bowie's request Crockett and several others carried the cot over the line, leaving Rose alone on the other side After its publication, several other eyewitnesses confirmed the account, but as Rose was deceased the story can only be authenticated by the word of the reporter, who admitted to embellishing other articles, "and thus many historians refuse to believe it."

Bowie ***perished with the rest of the Alamo defenders*** on March 6, when the Mexicans attacked. Most of the noncombatants in the fort, including Bowie's relatives, survived. Santa Anna ordered the alcalde of San Antonio, Francisco Antonio Ruiz, to confirm the identities of Bowie, Travis, and Crockett. After first ordering that Bowie be buried, as he was too brave a man to be burned like a dog, Santa Anna later had Bowie's body placed with those of the other Texians on the funeral pyre.

When Bowie's mother was informed of his death, she calmly stated, "I'll wager no wounds were found in his back." Various eyewitnesses to the battle gave conflicting accounts of Bowie's death. A newspaper article claimed that a Mexican soldier saw Bowie carried from his room on his cot, alive, after the conclusion of the battle. The soldier maintained that Bowie verbally castigated a Mexican officer in fluent Spanish, and the officer ordered Bowie's tongue cut out and his still-breathing body thrown onto the funeral pyre. This account has been disputed by numerous other witnesses, and it is thought to have been invented by the reporter.

Other witnesses maintained that they saw several Mexican soldiers enter Bowie's room, bayonet him, and carry him, alive, from the room. Various other stories circulated, with some witnesses claiming that Bowie shot himself and others saying he was killed by soldiers while too weak to lift his head. Alcalde Ruiz said that Bowie was found "dead in his bed." According to Wallace O Chariton,

The "most popular, and probably the most accurate" version is that Bowie died on his cot, "back braced against the wall, and using his pistols and his famous knife." One year after the battle, Juan Seguin returned to the Alamo and gathered the remaining ashes from the funeral pyre. He placed these in a coffin inscribed with the names of Bowie, Travis, and Crockett. The ashes were interred at the Cathedral of San Fernando.

Despite his continual pronouncements of wealth, Bowie's estate was found to be very small. His possessions were auctioned for only $99.50. His larger legacy is his position as "one of the legendary characters of the American frontier". Bowie left a "frustratingly sparse paper trail" of his life, and, for many, "where history failed, the legends prevailed." Although Bowie's name and his knife were well-known during his lifetime, his legend grew after October 1852, when ***DeBow's Review*** published an article written by his brother John Jones Bowie, called "Early Life in the Southwest—The Bowies."

The article focused primarily on the exploits of Jim Bowie. Beginning with that article, "romanticized stories" about Bowie began appearing in national press. In many cases, "these stories were pure melodrama, with Bowie rescuing some naïve planter's son or damsel in distress." Jim Bowie posthumously was inducted into the Blade Magazine Cutlery Hall of Fame at the 1988 Blade Show in Atlanta, Georgia in recognition for the impact that his eponymous design made upon generations of knife makers and cutlery companies.

***Both Bowie, Texas and Bowie County, Texas are named in honor of Jim Bowie.***

# JAMES HOWARD – STEAMBOAT BUILDER

GLENDY BURKE: Written by Stephen Foster in 1860 in honor of an actual steamboat that sank in 1855.

The Glendy Burke was built by James Howard, Born in Oldham, near Manchester, England who[1] left Britain in 1820 by sail boat accompanied by his parents and his younger brother.

After traveling by wagon to Wheeling (then in Virginia, now in West Virginia).They left Wheeling on a 'Flatboat' and arrived in Cincinnati. In Cincinatti his father John Howard, a weaver, set up a Mill. James was active in three of Cincinnnati's flourishing shipyards, first as a 'Jigger Boy' for William Gordon.

He carried water for and rations of spirits to the crews at work.

He then was employed by Burton Hazenand, as a ship's carpenter for William Bartshorn. James later became a Steamboat Builder and Founder of the Howard Shipyards in Jeffersonville, Indiana on the banks of the Ohio River (across the river from Louisville, Kentucky.)

Steamboats built by Howard included the "James Howard" and the second "Robert E. Lee." of Civil War Fame: the "Glendy Burke," the "General Buell" and the "Laurel Hill." From monument inscription:"

James Howard drowned October 14.1876 when his buggy rolled backward from a ferry into the river." He was 62 years old.[2] He was buried at Cave Hill in Louisville, Jefferson County, Kentucky, USA Plot: Section A, Lot 26

---

[1] Information obtained from a memorial at his graveside.

[2] Biography as a Steamboat builder by; Mike Hensley contributor to 'Find a Grave.'

## The Song

### THE GLENDY BURKE

De Glendy Burk is a mighty fast boat,
Wid a mighty fast captain too;
He sits up dah on de hurricane roof
And he keeps his eye on de crew.
I cant stay here, for dey work too hard;
I'm bound to leave dis town;
I'll take my duds and tote 'em on my back
When de Glendy Burk comes down.
*Chorus:*
Ho! for Lou'siana!
I'm bound to leave dis town;
I'll take my duds and tote 'em on my back
When de Glendy Burk comes down.

De Glendy Burk has a funny old crew
And dey sing de boatman's song,
Dey burn de pitch and de pine knot too,
For to shove de boat along.
De smoke goes up and de ingine roars
And de wheel goes round and round,
So fair you well! for I'll take a little ride
When de Glendy Burk comes down.
I'll work all night in de wind and storm,
I'll work all day in de rain,
Till I find myself on de levy dock
In New Orleans again.

Dey make me mow in de hay field here
And knock my head wid de flail,
I'll go wha dey work wid de sugar
And de cane And roll on de cotton bale.
My lady love is as pretty as a pink,
I'll meet her on de way
I'll take her back to de sunny old south
And dah I'll make her stay.
So dont you fret my honey dear,
Oh! dont you fret Miss Brown
I'll take you back 'fore de middle of de week
When de Glendy Burk comes down.

By Stephen C. Foster.

# STEPHEN COLLINS FOSTER

Stephen Collins Foster, of Irish descent, was born in Lawrenceville, now part of Pittsburgh, Pennsylvania. He was the youngest of ten children in a middle-class family that would eventually become nearly destitute after his father became an alcoholic. His parents were William Barclay Foster, merchant and trader, and Eliza Clayland Foster. Foster's parents ***were not musical.*** *One* of his first influences was his sister, Charlotte Susanna Foster, she played the piano and sang songs about loss and love.

He attended private academies in Allegheny, Athens, and Towanda. He received an education in English grammar, diction, the classics, penmanship, Latin and Greek, and mathematics. In 1839, Stephen Foster was sent to school at Athens Academy in Athens, Pennsylvania. His elder brother William, was serving his apprenticeship as an engineer at nearby Towanda, Pennsylvania and thought Stephen would benefit by being under his supervision.

Camptown, PA, the site of the ***Camptown Races***, is 30 miles from Athens, and 15 miles from Towanda. Stephen attended Athens Academy from 1839 to 1841. (The year after Stephen Foster left Athens Academy, it was destroyed by fire.)

His first composition, "Tioga Waltz", was written while he attended Athens Academy and performed at the commencement exercises for the year 1839. He was 14. ***It was not published during the composer's life time.***

His education included a brief period at Jefferson College (now Washington & Jefferson College) in Canonsburg, Pennsylvania, where his grandfather was once a trustee. His tuition was paid, but Foster had little spending money. Sources conflict on whether he left willingly or was dismissed, but either way, he left Canonsburg to visit Pittsburgh with another student and never returned.

Foster was influenced greatly by two men during his teenage years: Henry Kleber (1816–1897) and Dan Rice. The former was a classically trained musician who emigrated from the German city of Darmstadt and opened a music store in Pittsburgh, and who was among Stephen Foster's few formal music instructors. The latter was an entertainer—a clown and blackface singer, making his living in traveling circuses. Although respectful of the more civilized parlor songs of the day, he and his friends would often sit at a piano, writing and singing minstrel songs through the night. Eventually, Foster would learn to blend the two genres to write some of his best work.

## Career

In 1846, Foster moved to Cincinnati, Ohio and became a bookkeeper with his brother's steamship company. In Cincinnati, Foster penned his first successful songs, among them "Oh! Susanna". It would prove to be the anthem of the California Gold Rush in 1848–1849. In 1849, he published ***Foster's Ethiopian Melodies***, which included the successful song "Nelly Was a Lady", made famous by the Christy Minstrels.

He then returned to Pennsylvania and signed a contract with the Christy Minstrels. It was during this period that Foster would write most of his best-known songs: "Camptown Races" (1850), "Nelly Bly" (1850), "Old Folks at Home" (known also as "Swanee River", 1851), "My Old Kentucky Home" (1853), "Old Dog Tray" (1853), and "Jeanie With the Light Brown Hair" (1854), written for his wife Jane Denny McDowell.

Many of Foster's songs were of the blackface minstrel show tradition popular at the time. Foster sought, in his own words, to "build up taste... among refined people by making words suitable to their taste, instead of the trashy and really offensive words which belong to some songs of that order." He instructed Caucasian performers of his songs ***not to mock slaves*** but to get their audiences ***to feel compassion for them***.

Many of his songs had Southern themes, yet he had ***never lived in the South.*** He had **visited it only once,** by river-boat voyage (on his brother Dunning's steam boat, the ***James Millinger***) down the Mississippi to New Orleans, during his honeymoon in 1852...

Foster attempted to make a living as a professional songwriter. Foster realized very little of the profits which his works generated for sheet music printers. Multiple publishers often printed their own competing editions of Foster's tunes, not paying Foster anything. For "Oh, Susanna", ***he received $100.***

In 1860 he moved to New York City in 1860. A year later, his wife and daughter left him and returned to Pittsburgh. In 1862, his fortunes decreased, and as they did, ***so did the quality of his new songs***. Early in 1863, he began working with George Cooper, whose lyrics were often humorous and designed to appeal to musical theater audiences. The Civil War created a flurry of newly written music with patriotic war themes, but this did not benefit Foster.

## Death

He had been impoverished while living at the North American Hotel at 30 Bowery on the Lower East Side of Manhattan, New York.

His brother Henry described the accident that led to his death: Confined to bed for days by a persistent fever, Foster tried to call a chambermaid, but collapsed, falling against the washbasin next to his bed and shattering it, which gouged his head. It took three hours to get him to Bellevue Hospital, he succumbed three days after his admittance ***at the age of thirty-seven***. In his worn leather wallet there was found a scrap of paper that simply said "Dear friends and gentle hearts" along with 35 cents in Civil War scrip and ***three pennies***.

## Musical Compositions

"My Old Kentucky Home" (originally titled "Poor Uncle Tom, Good Night!", and sometimes also titled "My Old Kentucky Home, Good-Night!") is the state song of Kentucky.

It was published by Stephen Foster in 1853 and was adopted by the Kentucky General Assembly as the official state song on March 19, 1928. The song describes a scene of life on a slave plantation. The abolitionist Frederick Douglass believed the song ***was sympathetic to slaves***. In 1986, the Kentucky General Assembly adopted a version unlikely to cause offense in which the original word "darkies" was changed to "people."

The first draft of "My Old Kentucky Home" appeared in Stephen Collins Foster's workbook under the title "Poor Uncle Tom, Good Night." It was published in 1853 by New York's Firth, Pound, and Company.

According to folklore, Foster was inspired to write the song when, while traveling from his home in Pittsburgh, Pennsylvania to New Orleans, Louisiana, he ***(allegedly)*** stopped in Bardstown, Kentucky to visit his cousins, the Rowan family, and saw their magnificent Federal Hill mansion.

However, while Foster's trip to New Orleans is well-documented, ***his stop in Kentucky has not been conclusively substantiated.*** Also problematic is that ***the lyrics refer not to a mansion,*** but a "little cabin". Also, Foster's trip took place in 1852, after the first draft of the song had already been written. ***Foster's only documented trip to Kentucky occurred in 1833*** when his mother took him ***to visit relatives*** in Augusta and Louisville.
Another (***possibly more plausible***)[1] explanation holds that Foster was inspired by Harriet Beecher Stowe's novel ***Uncle Tom's Cabin***, which was published in 1851.

*MY OLD KENTUCKY HOME*
Original Lyrics (1853)

The sun shines bright in the old Kentucky home,
'Tis summer, the darkies are gay,
The corn top's ripe and the meadow's in the bloom
While the birds make music all the day.
The young folks roll on the little cabin floor,
All merry, all happy, and bright:
By'n by Hard Times comes a-knocking at the door,
Then my old Kentucky Home, good night.

Chorus:

Weep no more, my lady, oh! weep no more today!
We will sing a song for the old Kentucky Home,
For the old Kentucky Home, far away.

---

[1] As the lyrics referred to a little cabin, the theory that Foster adapted the song to the recent book "Uncle Tom's Cabin" would appear to lead in a more 'correct' direction. Whether he conscientiously or inadvertently was influenced by the book's theme is one of conjecture, if so it would appear to be a more plausible direction in which to place to origin of his inspiration to compose the song.

They hunt no more for the 'possum and the coon
On the meadow, the hill and the shore,
They sing no more by the glimmer of the moon,
On the bench by that old cabin door.
The day goes by like a shadow o'er the heart,
With sorrow where all was delight.
The time has come when the darkies have to part,
Then my old Kentucky home, good night!

*Chorus*

The head must bow and the back will have to bend,
Wherever the darkey may go:
A few more days and the trouble all will end
In the field where the sugar-canes may grow.
A few more days for to tote the weary load,
No matter 'twill never be light.
A few more days till we totter on the road,
Then my old Kentucky Home, good night.

*Chorus*

Contemporary Lyrics (1986)
(revised by House Resolution 159)[2]

The sun shines bright in My Old Kentucky Home,
'Tis summer, ***the people are gay;***
The corn-top's ripe and the meadow's in the bloom
While the birds make music all the day.
The young folks roll on the little cabin floor,
All merry, all happy and bright;
By 'n' by hard times comes a knocking at the door,
Then My Old Kentucky Home, good night!

***Chorus***
Weep no more my lady
Oh weep no more today;
We will sing one song
For My Old Kentucky Home
For My Old Kentucky Home, far away

[2] The revised version was adopted in 1986 due to a complaint suggesting that the song had discriminatory lyrics.

The young folks roll on the little cabin floor,
All merry, all happy and bright;
By 'n' by hard times comes a knocking at the door,
Then My Old Kentucky Home, good night!

***Chorus***
Weep no more my lady
Oh weep no more today;
We will sing one song
For My Old Kentucky Home
For My Old Kentucky Home, far away

# MARGARET FULLER

## May 23, 1810 – July 19, 1850

Known as Margaret Fuller, ***Sarah Margaret Fuller Ossol was b*****orn** Sarah **Margaret Fuller**, May 23rd 1810, Cambridgeport, Massachusetts. *She was a* journalist, critic and women's rights activist associated with the American transcendental movement[1] and the first full-time female book reviewer in journalism. Her book ***Woman in the Nineteenth Century*** is considered the first major feminist work in the United States.

---

[1] ***Transcendentalism*** was a group of new ideas in literature, religion, culture, and philosophy that emerged in New England in the 19th century.( Sometimes called ***American Transcendentalism*** to distinguish it from other uses of the word ***transcendental***.) It began as a protest against the general state of culture and society, in particular, the state of intellectualism at Harvard and the doctrine of the Unitarian church taught at Harvard Divinity School. Among transcendentalists' core beliefs was an ideal spiritual state that 'transcends' the physical and empirical and is only realized through the individual's intuition, rather than through the doctrines of established religions. Prominent transcendentalists included Ralph Waldo Emerson and Henry David Thoreau.

Margaret was the first child of Timothy Fuller and Margaret Crane Fuller. She was named after her paternal grandmother and her mother. At the age of nine, however, she dropped "Sarah" and insisted on being called "Margaret".

Her father taught Fuller to read and write He incorporated Latin into his teaching shortly after the birth of the couple's son, Eugene, in May 1815, and soon she was translating simple passages from Virgil

As a child, Margaret spent time with her mother daily, who taught her household chores and sewing. In 1817, her brother William Henry Fuller was born and her father was elected as a representative in the United States Congress. For the next eight years, he would spend four to six months of the year in Washington, D.C At the age of 10, Fuller wrote a cryptic note which her father saved: "On the 23rd of May, 1810, was born one foredoomed to sorrow and pain, and like others to have misfortunes"

At the advice of her aunts and uncles, in 1824 she was sent to the School for Young Ladies in Groton. Fuller left the Groton school and returned home at the age of 16 after having studied there for two years At home, she studied the classics and trained herself in several modern languages and various examples of world literature By this time, she realized ***she did not fit in with other young women her age.*** She wrote, "I have felt that I was not born to the common womanly lot". Eliza Farrar, wife of Harvard professor John Farrar and author of ***The Young Lady's Friend*** (1836), attempted to train her in feminine etiquette until the age of 20, though Farrar was never wholly successful.

She was an avid reader; by the time she was in her 30s, she had earned a reputation as the best-read person, male or female, in New England, and used her knowledge to give private lessons based on the teaching style of Elizabeth Palmer Peabody. Fuller hoped to earn her living through journalism and translation; her first published work, a response to historian George Bancroft, appeared in November 1834 in the ***North American Review.***

When she was 23, her father's law practice failed and he moved the family to a farm in Groton. On February 20, 1835, both Frederick Henry Hedge and James Freeman Clarke requested written contributions from her to publish in their respective periodicals.

Clarke helped her publish her first literary review in the ***Western Messenger*** in June: criticisms of recent biographies on George Crabbe and Hannah More.

In the fall of that year, she suffered a terrible migraine with a fever that lasted nine days; Fuller would often be plagued with headaches throughout her life. While she was still recovering, her father died of cholera on October 2, 1835 She was deeply affected by his death: "My father's image follows me constantly", she wrote. She vowed to step in as the head of the family and take care of her newly widowed mother and her younger siblings. Her father had not left a will, and two of her uncles gained control of his property and finances, later assessed at $18,098.15, and forced the family to rely on them for support. Humiliated by the way her uncles were treating the family, Fuller wrote that she regretted being "of the softer sex, and never more than now"

Fuller had hoped to prepare a biography of Johann Wolfgang von Goethe, but felt that she could work on it only if she traveled to Europe. Her father's death and her sudden responsibility over her family caused her to abandon this idea. In 1836, Fuller was given a job teaching at Bronson Alcott's Temple School in Boston, where she remained for a year. She then accepted an invitation to teach at the Greene Street School in Providence, Rhode Island, in April 1837 with the unusually high salary of $1,000 per year.

Her family sold the Groton farm and Fuller moved with them to Jamaica Plain, Massachusetts. On November 6, 1839, Fuller held the first of her "conversations", discussions among local women who met in the Boston home of the Peabodys Fuller intended these meetings to compensate for the lack of education for women with discussions and debates which focused on subjects including the fine arts, history, mythology, literature, and nature Serving as the "nucleus of conversation", Fuller also intended to answer the "great questions" facing women: "What were we born to do? How shall we do it? which so few ever propose to themselves 'till their best years are gone by".

A number of significant figures in the women's rights movement attended these "conversations", including Sophia Dana Ripley, Caroline Sturgis, and Maria White Lowell.

In October 1839, Ralph Waldo Emerson was seeking an editor for his transcendental journal ***The Dial*** and, after several had declined the role, he offered it to Fuller, referring to her as "my vivacious friend" Emerson had first met Fuller in Cambridge in 1835; of that meeting, he admitted "she made me laugh more than I liked".

The next summer, Fuller spent two weeks at Emerson's home in Concord where their friendship grew Fuller accepted Emerson's offer to edit *The Dial* on October 20, 1839, though she did not begin work until the first week of 1840. She edited the journal for the first two years of its existence from 1840 to 1842, though her promised annual salary of $200 was never paid.

Because of her role, she was soon recognized as one of the most important figures of the transcendental movement and was invited to George Ripley's Brook Farm communal experiment. Although she never officially joined the community, she became a frequent visitor often spending New Year's Eve there. In the summer of 1843, she traveled to Chicago, Milwaukee, Niagara Falls and Buffalo, New York; while there, she interacted with several Native Americans, including members of the Ottawa tribe and the Chippewa tribe. She reported her experiences in a book called ***Summer on the Lakes***, which she completed writing on her 34th birthday in 1844; critic Evert Augustus Duyckinck called it "the only genuine book, I can think of, this season" She had used the library at Harvard College for further background information on the Great Lakes region, making her the first woman allowed to use Harvard's library

Fuller left ***The Dial*** in 1844 in part because of ill health but also due to the publication's dwindling subscription list. She moved to New York that autumn and joined Horace Greeley's ***New York Tribune*** as literary critic, becoming the first full-time book reviewer in journalism and by 1846, was the publication's first female editor. Her first article, a review of a collection of essays by Emerson, was printed in the December 1, 1844, issue. At this time, the ***Tribune*** had some 50,000 subscribers and Fuller earned $500 a year for her work. In addition to American books, she reviewed foreign literature, concerts, lectures, and art exhibits. During her four years with the publication, she published more than 250 columns, most signed with a "*" as a byline

In these columns, Fuller discussed topics ranging from art and literature to political and social issues such as the plight of slaves and women's rights. She also published poetry; her poems, styled after the work of Emerson, do not have the same intellectual vigor as her criticism

At this time, she was also involved in a scandal involving fellow literary critic Edgar Allan Poe, who had been carrying on a public flirtation with the married poet Frances Sargent Osgood.At the same time, another poet, Elizabeth F. Ellet, became enamored of Poe and jealous of Osgood and suggested the relationship between Poe and Osgood was more than just innocent flirtation Osgood then sent Fuller and Anne Lynch Botta to Poe's cottage on her behalf to request that he return the personal letters she had sent him. Angered by their interference, Poe called them "Busy-bodies".A public scandal erupted and continued until Osgood's estranged husband Samuel Stillman Osgood stepped in and threatened to sue Ellet.

By the time she was in her 30s, Fuller had earned a reputation as the best-read person in New England, male or female, and became the first woman allowed to use the library at Harvard College. By the time she was in her 30s, Fuller had earned a reputation as the best-read person in New England, male or female, and became the first woman allowed to use the library at Harvard College.

One of Fuller's most important works, "The Great Lawsuit", was written in serial form for ***The Dial***. She originally intended to name the work "The Great Lawsuit: Man ***versus*** Men, Woman ***versus*** Women"; when it was expanded and published independently in 1845, it was instead named ***Woman in the Nineteenth Century***. After completing it, she wrote to a friend: "I had put a good deal of my true self in it, as if, I suppose I went away now, the measure of my footprint would be left on earth." The work discussed the role that women played in the American democracy and Fuller's opinion on possibilities for improvement. It has since become one of the major documents in American feminism and is considered the first of its kind in the United States. Her seminal work, ***Woman in the Nineteenth Century***, was published in 1845.

Fuller was sent to Europe in 1846 by the ***New York Tribune***, specifically England and Italy, as its ***first female foreign correspondent***. She traveled from Boston to Liverpool in August on the ***Cambria***, a vessel that used both sail and steam to make the journey in ten days and sixteen hours. Over the next four years she provided thirty-seven reports from overseas. She interviewed many prominent writers including George Sand and Thomas Carlyle—whom she found disappointing because of his reactionary politics, among other things. George Sand had previously been an idol of hers, but Fuller was disappointed when Sand chose not to run for the French National Assembly, ***saying that women were not ready to vote or to hold political office***. Fuller was also given a letter of introduction from Cornelius Mathews for Elizabeth Barrett; the two women did not meet, as Barrett had just eloped with Robert Browning.

In the spring of 1846, she met Giuseppe Mazzini in England, who had been in exile from Italy since 1837. Fuller also met the Italian revolutionary Giovanni Angelo Ossoli, a marquis who had been disinherited by his family because of his support for Mazzini. Fuller and Ossoli moved in together in Florence, Italy, likely before they were married, if they ever were. Fuller originally did not support marrying him, in part because of their different religions; she was Protestant and he was Roman Catholic. Emerson speculated that the couple was "married perhaps in Oct. Nov. or Dec" of 1847, though he did not explain his reasoning.

Biographers have speculated that the couple married on April 4, 1848, to celebrate the anniversary of their first meeting. By the time the couple moved to Florence, they were referred to as husband and wife, though it is unclear if any formal ceremony took place.It seems certain that at the time their child was born, they were not married. By New Year's Day 1848, she suspected that she was pregnant but kept it from Ossoli for several weeks. Their child, Angelo Eugene Philip Ossoli, was born in early September 1848; they nicknamed him Angelino. The couple was very secretive about their relationship but, after Angelino suffered an unnamed illness, they became closer. Fuller finally informed her mother about Ossoli and Angelino in August 1849. The letter explained that she had kept silent so as not to upset her "but it has become necessary, on account of the child, for us to live publicly and permanently together."

Her mother's response makes it clear that she was aware that a legal marriage had not taken place.even so, she was happy for her daughter, writing: "I send my first kiss with my fervent blessing to my grandson." Modern biographers are still unclear if Fuller and Ossoli ever married.

The couple supported Giuseppe Mazzini's revolution for the establishment of a Roman Republic in 1849—Ossoli fought in the struggle while Fuller volunteered at a supporting hospital. After generations of rule by several parties, few of which were Italian, Italy had been left without an official central government with various pieces of the country overseen by different weak governments, including one under the control of the Papacy.

When Pope Pius IX was appointed in 1846, he made small steps towards the establishment of a central Italian democratic government, though revolutionaries like Mazzini did not trust the Pope's efforts. The political unrest was enough that the Pope disguised himself and escaped on November 24, 1848. A Roman republic with a representative government was established in February 1849, only to be destroyed by an invasion from France a few months later because Fuller and Ossoli were aligned with the revolution, when Pope Pius IX returned to Rome in 1850.

They had to flee Italy and decided to move to the United States.she intended to use her experience to write a book about the history of the Roman Republic, a work she may have begun as early as 1847,[I] hoping to find an American publisher after a British one rejected it. She believed the work would be her most important, referring to it in a March 1849 letter to her brother Richard as, "something good ***which may survive my troubled existence***."

In the beginning of the year 1850, Fuller wrote to a friend: "It has long seemed that in the year 1850 I should stand on some important plateau in the ascent of life... I feel however no marked and important change as yet." Also that year, Fuller wrote: "I ***am absurdly fearful and various omens have combined to give me a dark feeling... It seems to me that my future upon earth will soon close... I have a vague expectation of some crisis—I know not what***". A few days after writing this, Fuller, Ossoli, and their child began a five-week return voyage to the United States aboard the ship Elizabeth.

The ship was an American merchant freighter carrying cargo that included mostly marble from Carrara as well as a statue of John C. Calhoun sculpted by Hiram Powers.,after a short delay due to rain, the ***Elizabeth*** set sail on May 17.at sea, the ship's captain, Seth Hasty, died of smallpox. The child, Angelino, contracted the disease as well, though he recovered.

Possibly because of the inexperienced first mate, now serving as captain, the ***ship slammed into a sandbar*** less than 100 yards from Fire Island, New York, on July 19, 1850, around 3:30 a.m. Many of the other passengers and crew members abandoned ship. The first mate, Mr. Bangs, urged Fuller and Ossoli to try ***to save themselves and their child*** as ***he jumped overboard*** later claiming he believed Fuller had wanted to be left behind to die.

On the beach, people arrived with carts hoping to take advantage if any cargo washed to shore; ***none made any effort to rescue the crew or passengers of the Elizabeth*** though ***they were only 50 yards from shore***. Ossoli and Fuller, along with their child, were some of the last on the ship; most others had attempted to swim to shore. Eventually, Ossoli was thrown overboard by a massive wave and, after the wave had passed, a crewman who witnessed the event said Fuller could not be seen. ***Fuller's body was never recovered.***

Henry David Thoreau traveled to New York, at the urging of Emerson, to search the shore but neither Fuller's body nor that of her husband were ever recovered; only her child Angelino ***had washed ashore***. Few of their possessions were found other than some of the child's clothes and a few letters. ***Fuller's manuscript on the history of the Roman Republic was also lost***. A memorial to Fuller was erected on the beach at Fire Island in 1901 through the efforts of Julia Ward Howe.

## A Memorial

A cenotaph to Fuller and Ossoli, under which Angelino is buried, is in Mount Auburn Cemetery, Cambridge, Massachusetts. The inscription reads, in part:

> ***By birth a child of New England***
> ***By adoption a citizen of Rome***
> ***By genius belonging to the world***

Within a week after her death, Horace Greeley suggested to Emerson that a biography of Fuller, to be called ***Margaret and Her Friends***, be prepared quickly "before the interest excited by her sad decease has passed away". Many of her writings were soon collected together by her brother Arthur as ***At Home and Abroad*** (1856) and ***Life Without and Life Within*** (1858).

He also edited a new version of ***Woman in the Nineteenth Century*** in 1855. In February 1852, ***The Memoirs of Margaret Fuller Ossoli*** was published edited by Emerson, James Freeman Clarke, and William Henry Channing, though much of the work was censored or reworded. It particularly left out details about her love affair with Ossoli and an earlier relationship with a man named James Nathan.

The three editors, believing the public interest in Fuller would be short-lived and that she would not survive as a historical figure, were not concerned about accuracy Even so, for a time, ***it was the best-selling biography of the decade and went through thirteen editions before the end of the century***.The book focused on her personality rather than her work and, as a result, detractors of the book ignored her status as a critic and instead criticized her personal life and her "unwomanly" arrogance.

Fuller was an advocate of women's rights and, in particular, women's education and the right to employment. She also encouraged many other reforms in society, including prison reform and the emancipation of slaves in the United States. Many other advocates for women's rights and feminism, including Susan B. Anthony, cite Fuller as a source of inspiration.

Fuller was an early proponent of feminism and especially believed in providing education to women. Once equal educational rights were afforded women, she believed, women could push for equal political rights as well. She advocated that women ***seek any employment they wish***, rather than catering to the stereotypical "feminine" roles of the time, such as teaching.She once said, "If you ask me what office women should fill, I reply—***any... let them be sea captains if you will***. I do not doubt that there are women well fitted for such an office"

She had great confidence in all women but doubted that a woman would produce a lasting work of art or literature in her time and disliked the popular female poets of her time. Fuller also warned women to be careful about marriage and not to become dependent on their husbands.

As she wrote, "I wish woman to live, ***first*** for God's sake. Then she will not make an imperfect man for her god, and thus sink to idolatry. Then she will not take what is not fit for her from a sense of weakness and poverty" By 1832, she had made a personal commitment to stay single .

Fuller also questioned a definitive line between male and female: "There is no wholly masculine man... no purely feminine" but that both were present in any individual. She suggested also that within a female were two parts: the intellectual side (which she called the Minerva) and the "lyrical" or "Femality" side (the Muse) She admired the work of Emanuel Swedenborg, who believed men and women shared "an angelic ministry", as she wrote, as well as Charles Fourier, who placed "Woman on an entire equality with Man" Unlike several contemporary women writers, including "Mrs. Sigourney" and "Mrs. Stowe", she was familiarly referred to in a less formal manner as "Margaret"

Fuller also advocated reform at all levels of society, including prison. In October 1844, she visited Sing Sing and interviewed the women prisoners, even staying overnight in the facility. Sing Sing was developing a more humane system for its women inmates, many of whom were prostitutes. Fuller was also concerned about the homeless and those living in dire poverty, especially in New York.

She also admitted that, though she was raised to believe "that the Indian obstinately refused to be civilized", her travels in the American West made her realize that the white man unfairly treated the Native Americans; she considered Native Americans an important part of American heritage,she also supported the rights of African-Americans, referring to "this cancer of slavery".

She suggested that those who were interested in the Abolition movement follow the same reasoning when considering the rights of women: "As the friend of the Negro assumes that one man cannot by right hold another in bondage, so should the Friend of Woman assume that Man cannot by right lay even well-meant restrictions on Woman." She suggested that those who spoke against the emancipation of slaves were similar to those who did not support the emancipation of Italy.

She agreed with the transcendental concern for the psychological well-being of the individual, though she was never comfortable being labeled a transcendentalist. Even so, she wrote, if being labeled a transcendentalist means "that I have an active mind frequently busy with large topics I hope it is so"

She criticized people like Emerson, however, for focusing too much on individual improvement and not enough on social reform like other members of the so-called Transcendental Club, she rebelled against the past and believed in the possibility of change. However, unlike others in the movement, her rebellion was not based on religion.

Fuller was especially known in her time for her personality and, in particular, for being overly self-confident and having a bad temper This personality was the inspiration for the character Hester Prynne in Nathaniel Hawthorne's novel ***The Scarlet Letter***, specifically her radical thinking about "the whole race of womanhood" She may also be the basis for the character Zenobia in another of Hawthorne's works, ***The Blithedale Romance*** Hawthorne and his then-fiancée Sophia had first met Fuller in October 1839.

She was also an inspiration to poet Walt Whitman, who believed in her call for the forging of a new national identity and a truly American literature. Elizabeth Barrett Browning was also a strong admirer, but believed that Fuller's unconventional views were ***unappreciated in the United States and, therefore, she was better off dead***. She also said that Fuller's history of the Roman Republic would have been her greatest work: "The work she was preparing upon Italy would probably have been more equal to her faculty than anything previously produced by her pen (her other writings being curiously inferior to the impressions her conversation gave you)"

An 1860 essay collection, ***Historical Pictures Retouched***, by Caroline Healey Dall, called Fuller's ***Woman in the Nineteenth Century*** "doubtless the most brilliant, complete, and scholarly statement ever made on the subject" despite his personal issues with Fuller, the typically harsh literary critic Edgar Allan Poe wrote of the work as "a book which few women in the country could have written, and no woman in the country would have published, with the exception of Miss Fuller", noting its "independence" and "unmitigated radicalism".

Thoreau also thought highly of the book, suggesting that its strength came in part from Fuller's conversational ability. As he called it, it was "rich extempore writing, talking with pen in hand"

Another admirer was Susan B. Anthony, a pioneer of women's rights, who wrote that Fuller "possessed more influence on the thought of American women than any woman previous to her time". Fuller's work may have partially inspired the Seneca Falls Convention in 1848. Anthony, along with Elizabeth Cady Stanton and Matilda Joslyn Gage wrote in their ***History of Woman Suffrage*** that Fuller "was the precursor of the Women's Rights agitation"

Modern scholars have suggested ***Woman in the Nineteenth Century*** was the first major women's rights work since Mary Wollstonecraft's ***A Vindication of the Rights of Woman*** (1792) though an early comparison between the two women came from George Eliot in 1855
It is unclear if Fuller was familiar with Wollstonecraft's works; in her childhood, her father prevented her from reading them In 1995, Fuller was inducted into the National Women's Hall of Fame.

## Critics of her works

The influential editor Rufus Wilmot Griswold, who believed she went against his notion of feminine modesty, referred to ***Woman in the Nineteenth Century*** as "an eloquent expression of her discontent at having been created female." New York writer Charles Frederick Briggs said that she was "wasting the time of her readers", especially because she was an unmarried woman and therefore could not "truly represent the female character."

English writer and critic Matthew Arnold scoffed at Fuller's conversations as well, saying, "My G–d, what rot did she and the other female dogs of Boston talk about Greek mythology!" Sophia Hawthorne, who had previously been a supporter of Fuller, was critical of her after ***Woman of the Nineteenth Century*** was published:

The impression it left was disagreeable. I did not like the tone of it—& did not agree with her at all about the change in woman's outward circumstances... Neither do I believe in such a character of man as she gives. It is altogether too ignoble. I think Margaret speaks of many things that should not be spoken of.

Fuller had angered fellow poet and critic James Russell Lowell when she reviewed his work, calling him "absolutely wanting in the true spirit and tone of poesy... his verse is stereotyped, his thought sounds no depth; and posterity will not remember him." In response, Lowell took revenge in his satirical ***A Fable for Critics***, first published in October 1848.

At first, he considered excluding her entirely but ultimately gave her what was called the "most wholly negative characterization" in the work. Referring to her as Miranda, Lowell wrote that she stole old ideas and presented them as her own, she was genuine only in her spite and "when acting as censor, she privately blows a censer of vanity 'neath her own nose".

Shortly after Fuller's death, her importance faded. Her obituary in the newspaper she had once edited, the ***Daily Tribune***, said that her works had a few great sentiments, "but as a whole they must commend themselves mainly by their vigor of thought and habitual fearlessness rather than freedom of utterance"

In the 20th century, American writer Elizabeth Hardwick, former wife of Robert Lowell, wrote an essay called "The Genius of Margaret Fuller" (1986). She compared her own move from Boston to New York to Fuller's, saying that Boston was not a good place for intellectuals, despite the assumption that it was the best place for intellectuals

# SARAH JOSEPHA HALE

**October 24, 1788 - April 30, 1879**

Sarah Josepha Hale was born in Newport, New Hampshire to Captain Gordon Buell and Martha Whittlesay Buell. Early in her life, she was educated by her mother and her brother Horatio who taught her what he had learned at Dartmouth; later on, Hale was an ***autodidact***.[1]

While working as a schoolteacher in 1811, her father opened a tavern called The Rising Sun in Newport; she met David Hale the same year. The couple married at The Rising Sun, on October 23, 1813, and had five children: David (1815), Horatio (1817), Frances (1819), Sarah (1820), William (1822) David Hale, a lawyer, died in 1822 after his death , Sarah Josepha Hale ***wore black for the rest of her life***.

---

[1] An ***autodidact*** is a mostly self-taught person, as opposed to learning in a school setting or from a full-time tutor or mentor.A person may become an autodidact at nearly any point in his or her life. While some may have been educated in a conventional manner in a particular field, they may choose to educate themselves in other, often unrelated areas.

In 1823, with the monetary support of her (then late) husband's Freemason lodge, she published a collection of her poems entitled ***The Genius of Oblivion.***

She famously campaigned for the creation of the American holiday known as Thanksgiving. Sarah became famous as the author of the nursery rhyme "Mary Had a Little Lamb". The nursery rhyme was first ***published*** (as opposed to ***written***) as an original poem by Sarah Josepha Hale on May $24^{th}$ 1830 and was inspired by an actual incident.

As a girl, Mary Sawyer (later Mrs. Mary Tyler) kept a pet lamb, which she took to school one day at the suggestion of her brother. A commotion naturally ensued. Mary recalled:

"Visiting school that morning was a young man by the name of John Roulstone, a nephew of the Reverend Lemuel Capen, who was then settled in Sterling. It was the custom then for students to prepare for college with ministers, and for this purpose Mr. Roulstone was studying with his uncle. The young man was very much pleased with the incident of the lamb; and the next day he rode across the fields on horseback to the little old schoolhouse and handed me a slip of paper which had written upon it the three original stanzas of the poem."

***MARY HAD A LITTLE LAMB***

Mary had a little lamb,
little lamb, little lamb,
Mary had a little lamb,
whose fleece was white as snow.
And everywhere that Mary went,
Mary went, Mary went,
and everywhere that Mary went,
the lamb was sure to go.

It followed her to school one day
school one day, school one day,
It followed her to school one day,
which was against the rules.
It made the children laugh and play,
laugh and play, laugh and play,
it made the children laugh and play
to see a lamb at school.

And so the teacher turned it out,
turned it out, turned it out,
And so the teacher turned it out,
but still it lingered near,
And waited patiently about,
patiently about, patiently about,
And waited patiently about
till Mary did appear.

"Why does the lamb love Mary so?"
Love Mary so? Love Mary so?
"Why does the lamb love Mary so,"
the eager children cry.
"Why, Mary loves the lamb, you know."
The lamb, you know, the lamb, you know,
"Why, Mary loves the lamb, you know,"
the teacher did reply.

In the 1830s, Lowell Mason set the nursery rhyme to a melody adding repetition in the verses[2]:

Her novel, published in the U.S. under the title ***Northwood: Life North and South*** and in London under the title, ***A New England Tale***, made her one of the first American women novelists and one of the first of either gender to write a book about slavery.

The book, which espoused New England virtues as the model to follow for national prosperity, was immediately successful. The novel not only espoused New England values, but supported the re-Africanization of slaves in the colony of Liberia. It is an argument for Thomas Jefferson's apprehension regarding the difficulty the races would encounter (and have encountered) in living together with the specter of slavery between them.

[2] There are two competing theories on the origin of this poem. One holds that Roulstone wrote the first four lines and that the final twelve lines, more moralistic and much less childlike than the first, were composed by Sarah Josepha Hale; the other is that Hale was responsible for the entire poem. Another person who claims to have written the poem and well known nursery rhyme is Mary Hughs but ***it has been confirmed that Sarah Hale wrote it.***

## Northwood: Life North and South (1852)

In her introduction to the second edition (1852) Sarah Hale writes in the spirit that is characteristic of the principles by which she lived, "The great error of those who would sever the Union rather than see a slave within its borders, is, that they forget the master is their brother, as well as the servant; and that the spirit which seeks to do good to all and evil to none is the only true Christian philanthropy." The premise of her book is just that. While slavery hurts and dehumanizes slaves absolutely, it also dehumanizes the masters and retards the psychological, moral and technological progress of their world.

The book garnered praise from Reverend John Blake, who asked Hale to move to Boston to serve as the editor of his journal, ***Ladies' Magazine***. She agreed and, from 1828 until 1836, she served as editor in Boston, though she preferred being called an "editress". Hale hoped the magazine would help in educating women, as she wrote, "not that they may usurp the situation, or encroach on the prerogatives of man; but that each individual may lend her aid to the intellectual and moral character of those within her sphere."

Her collection ***Poems for Our Children***, which includes the now-famous "Mary Had a Little Lamb", was published in 1830, though its original title was "Mary's Lamb".The poem was intentionally written for children, an audience for which many women poets of this period were writing.Hale founded the Seaman's Aid Society in 1833 to assist the surviving families of Boston sailors who died at sea.Louis Antoine Godey of Philadelphia wanted to hire Hale as the editor of his journal ***Godey's Lady's Book***.

He bought the ***Ladies' Magazine***, now renamed ***American Ladies' Magazine***, and merged it with his journal. In 1837 Hale began working as editor of the expanded ***Godey's Lady's Book*** but insisted she edit from Boston while her youngest son, William, attended Harvard College.

She remained editor at ***Godey's*** for forty years, retiring almost at the age of ninety in 1877.During this time, she became one of the most important and influential arbiters of American taste. In its day, ***Godey's***, with no significant competitors, had an influence unimaginable for any single publication today. The magazine is credited with an ability to influence fashions not only for women's clothes, but also in domestic architecture.

## Thanksgiving

Hale is credited as the individual most responsible for making Thanksgiving ***a national holiday*** in the United States; previously celebrated only in New England. Each state scheduled its own holiday, some as early as October and others as late as January; it was largely unknown in the American South. Her advocacy for the national holiday began in 1846 and lasted 17 years before it was successful.In support of the proposed national holiday, she wrote letters to five Presidents of the United States -- Zachary Taylor, Millard Filmore, Franklin Pierce, James Buchanan, and Abraham Lincoln. Her initial letters failed to persuade, but the letter she wrote to Lincoln did convince him to support legislation establishing a national holiday of Thanksgiving in 1863. The new national holiday was considered a ***unifying day after the stress of the American Civil War***.Prior to the addition of Thanksgiving, the only national holidays celebrated in the United States were Washington's Birthday and Independence Day.

Hale, was a successful and popular editor, and was respected as an arbiter of taste for middle-class women in matters of fashion, cooking, literature, and morality.In her work, however, she was reinforcing stereotypical gender roles, specifically domestic roles for women and celebrated the "separate sphere" for women while casually trying to expand on it.

For example, she believed that women shaped the morals of society, and pushed for women to write morally uplifting novels. She wrote that "while the ocean of political life is heaving and raging with the storm of partisan passions among the men of America... [***women as]*** the true conservators of peace and good-will, should be careful to cultivate every gentle feeling". She did not support women's suffrage and instead believed in the "secret, silent influence of women" to sway men voters.

She was an advocate for education, and supported play and physical education as valuable learning experiences for children. She wrote in 1829 that "Physical health and its attendant cheerfulness promote a happy tone of moral feeling, and they are indispensable to successful intellectual effort.An early supporter of women's education, particularly higher education for women. She helped in the founding of Vassar College.Her championship of education for women began with her editorship of the ***Ladies' Magazine*** and continued until she retired.

She wrote no fewer than seventeen articles and editorials devoted to the subject of women's education, and is credited with helping make the founding of an all-women's college acceptable to a public unaccustomed to the idea.

Her efforts in promoting women's education were rewarded in 1860 when the Baltimore Female College awarded her a medal "for distinguished services in the cause of female education".As an editor, she created a section headed "Employment for Women" beginning in 1852 discussing women's attempts to enter the workforce

.She also published the works of Catharine Beecher, Emma Willard and other early advocates of education for women.Hale noted that American writers were often overlooked in the 1820s and 1830s, by American magazines who often merely compiled and reprinted articles from British periodicals, she was part of a group of several American editors who insisted on publishing American writers. In practical terms, this meant that she sometimes personally wrote half of the material published in the *Ladies' Magazine*. In later years, it meant that she particularly liked to publish fiction with American themes, the frontier, and historical fiction set during the American Revolution.

She adamantly opposed slavery, but she was equally devoted to the Union. She campaigned in her pages for a unified American culture and nation, frequently running stories in which southerners and northerners fought together against the British, or in which a southerner and a northerner fell in love and married.Hale retired from editorial duties in 1877 at the age of 89.

The same year, Thomas Edison spoke the opening lines of "Mary's Lamb": the first ever recorded on his newly invented phonograph. Hale died at her home, 1413 Locust Street in Philadelphia, on April 30, 1879.

# HARRIET BEECHER STOWE

Harriet Beecher Stowe was an American abolitionist and author. Stowe's novel ***Uncle Tom's Cabin*** (1852) depicted life for African-Americans under slavery; it reached millions as a novel and play, and became influential in the U.S. and Britain and made the ***political issues of the 1850s*** regarding slavery tangible to millions, ***energizing anti-slavery forces in the American North***, while ***provoking widespread anger in the South***. Upon meeting Stowe, Abraham Lincoln allegedly remarked, "So you're the little lady who started this great war!"The quote is regarded as apocryphal.

Published in 1852, the novel had a profound effect on attitudes toward African Americans and slavery in the United States, so much in the latter case that ***the novel intensified the sectional conflict leading to the American Civil War.***

Stowe, a Connecticut-born preacher at the Hartford Female Academy and an active abolitionist, focused the novel on the character of Uncle Tom, a long-suffering slave around whom the stories of other characters both fellow slaves and slave owners revolve. The sentimental novel depicts the reality of slavery while also asserting that Christian love can overcome something as destructive as enslavement of fellow human beings.

Stowe, a Connecticut-born teacher at the Hartford Female Academy and an active abolitionist, wrote the novel as a response to the 1850 passage of the second Fugitive Slave Act (which punished those who aided runaway slaves and diminished the rights of fugitives as well as freed slaves

She was partly inspired to create ***Uncle Tom's Cabin*** by the autobiography of Josiah Henson, a slave who lived and worked on a 3,700 acre tobacco plantation in North Bethesda, Maryland owned by Isaac Riley.

Henson escaped slavery in 1830 by fleeing to the Province of Upper Canada (***now Ontario***)[1] where he helped other fugitive slaves arrive and become self-sufficient, and there he wrote his memoirs. Stowe eventually acknowledged that Henson's writings ***inspired Uncle Tom's Cabin***. When Stowe's work became a best-seller, Henson republished his memoirs as ***The Memoirs of Uncle Tom***, and traveled extensively in the United States and Europe.

Most of the book was composed in Brunswick, Maine, where her husband, Calvin Ellis Stowe, taught at his alma mater, Bowdoin College. Her portrayal of a long-suffering slave, (***Uncle Tom***) ***stoked the embers of the abolitionist cause who fully supported it*** which fueled the fire of the abolitionists.

In it's first year of publication, the book sold 300,000 copies (within the United States alone) the success and the impact this book had on the nation was of such impact that when Abraham Lincoln met Stowe at the start of the Civil War, he was (***allegedly***) quoted as saying "So this is the little lady who made this big war."

***Uncle Tom's Cabin*** first appeared as a 40-week serial in ***National Era***, an abolitionist periodical, in June 5, 1851. Jewett commissioned Hammatt Billings to produce the six fullpage illustrations for the first printing. Published in book form, March 20th 1852, the novel soon sold out its complete print run. A number of other editions were soon printed (including a deluxe edition in 1853, featuring 117 illustrations by Billings). In its first year of publication, 300,000 copies of ***Uncle Tom's Cabin*** were sold. The book was translated into all major languages, and eventually became the ***second best-selling book after the Bible***.

---

[1] Stowe's novel lent its name to Henson's home—Uncle Tom's Cabin Historic Site, near Dresden, in southwestern Ontario (near the cities of Windsor and Detroit. Michigan). Dresden, Ontario has a museum open since the 1940's. ( The original cabin where Henson lived while he was a slave still exists in Montgomery County, Maryland. and is part of the National Park Service National Underground Railroad Network to Freedom program.. Stowe also said she based the novel on a number of interviews with escaped slaves at the when Stowe lived in Cincinnati, Ohio, across the Ohio River from Kentucky,(Then a slave state) In Cincinnati the Underground Railroad had local abolitionist sympathizers and was active in assistiing runaway slaves on their escape route.

## Overview of the Novel

***Eliza escapes with her son, Tom sold "down the river".***

The book opens with a Kentucky farmer named Arthur Shelby facing the loss of his farm because of debts. Even though he and his wife, Emily Shelby, believe that they have a benevolent relationship with their slaves, Shelby decides to raise the needed funds by selling two of them—Uncle Tom, a middle-aged man with a wife and children, and Harry, the son of Emily Shelby's maid Eliza—to a slave trader. Emily Shelby hates the idea of doing this because she had promised her maid that her child would never be sold; Emily's son, George Shelby, hates to see Tom go because he sees the man as his friend and mentor.When Eliza overhears Mr. and Mrs. Shelby discussing plans to sell Tom and Harry, Eliza determines to run away with her son. The novel states that Eliza made this decision because she fears losing her only surviving child (she had already miscarried two children). Eliza departs that night, leaving a note of apology to her mistress.

While all of this is happening, Uncle Tom is sold and placed on a riverboat, which sets sail down the Mississippi River. While on board, Tom meets and befriends a young white girl named Eva. When Eva falls into the river, Tom saves her. In gratitude, Eva's father, Augustine St. Clare, buys Tom from the slave trader and takes him with the family to their home in New Orleans. During this time, Tom and Eva begin to relate to one another because of the deep Christian faith they both share.

***Eliza's family hunted, Tom's life with St. Clare.***

During Eliza's escape, she meets up with her husband George Harris, who had run away previously. They decide to attempt to reach Canada. However, they are now being tracked by a slave hunter named Tom Loker. Eventually Loker and his men trap Eliza and her family, causing George to shoot Loker. Worried that Loker may die, Eliza convinces George to bring the slave hunter to a nearby Quaker settlement for medical treatment.

Back in New Orleans, St. Clare debates slavery with his Northern cousin Ophelia who, while opposing slavery, is prejudiced against black people. St. Clare, however, believes he is not biased, even though he is a slave owner.

In an attempt to show Ophelia that her views on blacks are wrong, St. Clare purchases Topsy, a young black slave. St. Clare then asks Ophelia to educate her.

After Tom has lived with the St. Clares for two years, Eva grows very ill. Before she dies she experiences a vision of heaven, which she shares with the people around her. As a result of her death and vision, the other characters resolve to change their lives, with Ophelia promising to throw off her personal prejudices against blacks, Topsy saying she will better herself, and St. Clare pledging to free Uncle Tom.

Cassy, another of Legree's slaves, is shown ministering to Uncle Tom after his whipping. Before St. Clare can follow through on his pledge, however, he dies after being stabbed while entering a New Orleans tavern.

His wife reneges on her late husband's vow and sells Tom at auction to a vicious plantation owner named Simon Legree. Legree (a transplanted northerner) takes Tom to rural Louisiana, where Tom meets Legree's other slaves, including Emmeline (whom Legree purchased at the same time). Legree begins to hate Tom when Tom refuses Legree's order to whip his fellow slave. Legree beats Tom viciously, and resolves to crush his new slave's faith in God. Despite Legree's cruelty, however, Tom refuses to stop reading his Bible and comforting the other slaves as best he can. While at the plantation, Tom meets Cassy, another of Legree's slaves. Cassy was previously separated from her son and daughter when they were sold; unable to endure the pain of seeing another child sold, she killed her third child.

At this point Tom Loker returns to the story. Loker has changed as the result of being healed by the Quakers. George, Eliza, and Harry have also obtained their freedom after crossing into Canada. In Louisiana, Uncle Tom almost succumbs to hopelessness, as his faith in God is tested by the hardships of the plantation. However, he has two visions, one of Jesus and one of Eva, which renew his resolve to remain a faithful Christian, even unto death. He encourages Cassy to escape, which she does, taking Emmeline with her. When Tom refuses to tell Legree where Cassy and Emmeline have gone, Legree orders his overseers to kill Tom. As Tom is dying, he forgives the overseers who savagely beat him. Humbled by the character of the man they have killed, both men become Christians. Very shortly before Tom's death, George Shelby (Arthur Shelby's son) arrives to buy Tom’s freedom, but finds he is too late.

## Final section

On their boat ride to freedom, Cassy and Emmeline meet George Harris' sister and accompany her to Canada. Once there, Cassy discovers that Eliza is her long-lost daughter who was sold as a child. Now that their family is together again, they travel to France and eventually Liberia, the African nation created for former American slaves. There they meet Cassy's long-lost son. George Shelby returns to the Kentucky farm and frees all his slaves. George tells them to remember Tom's sacrifice and his belief in the true meaning of Christianity.

Uncle Tom, the title character, was initially seen as a noble, long-suffering Christian slave. In more recent years, however, his name has become an epithet directed towards African-Americans who are accused of selling out to whites (for more on this, see the creation and popularization of stereotypes section). Stowe intended Tom to be a "noble hero" and praiseworthy person. Throughout the book, far from allowing himself to be exploited, Tom stands up for his beliefs and is grudgingly admired even by his enemies.

## Eliza

A slave (personal maid to Mrs. Shelby), she escapes to the North with her five-year old son Harry after he is sold to Mr. Haley. Her husband, George, eventually finds Eliza and Harry in Ohio, and emigrates with them to Canada, then France and finally Liberia.

The character Eliza was inspired by an account given at Lane Theological Seminary in Cincinnati by John Rankin to Stowe's husband Calvin, a professor at the school. According to Rankin, in February, 1838 a young slave woman had escaped across the frozen Ohio River to the town of Ripley with her child in her arms and stayed at his house on her way further north.

## Eva

Eva, whose real name is Evangeline St. Clare, is the daughter of Augustine St. Clare. Eva enters the narrative when Uncle Tom is traveling via steamship to New Orleans to be sold, and he rescues the 5 or 6 year-old girl from drowning. Eva begs her father to buy Tom, and he becomes the head coachman at the St. Clare plantation.

He spends most of his time with the angelic Eva, however. Eva constantly talks about love and forgiveness, even convincing the dour slave girl Topsy that she deserves love. She even touches the heart of her sour aunt, Ophelia.Eventually Eva falls terminally ill. Before dying, she gives a lock of her hair to each of the slaves, telling them that they must become Christians so that they may see each other in Heaven. On her deathbed, she convinces her father to free Tom, but because of circumstances the promise never materializes.A similar character, also named ***Little Eva***, later appeared in the children's novel ***Little Eva: The Flower of the South*** by Philip J. Cozans (although this ironically was an anti-Tom novel).
To a certain degree, the Little Eva portrayed by Cozans could be the same Eva introduced by Stowe.

## Simon Legree

A cruel slave owner—a Northerner by birth—whose name has become synonymous with greed. His goal is to demoralize Tom and break him of his religious faith; he eventually beats Tom to death out of frustration for his slave's unbreakable belief in God. The novel reveals that, as a young man, he had abandoned his sickly mother for a life at sea, and ignored her letter to see her one last time at her deathbed. He sexually exploits Cassie, who despises him, and later sets his designs on Emmeline.

## Other characters

There are a number of secondary and minor characters in ***Uncle Tom's Cabin***. Among the more notable are:

**Arthur Shelby**, Tom's master in Kentucky. Shelby is characterized as a "kind" slaveowner and a stereotypical Southern gentleman.

**Emily Shelby**, Arthur Shelby's wife. A deeply religious woman who strives to be a kind and moral influence upon her slaves. She is appalled when her husband sells his slaves with a slave trader. As a woman, she has no legal way to stop this, as all property belongs to her husband.

**George Shelby**, Arthur and Emily's son, who sees Tom as a "friend" and as the perfect Christian.

**Augustine St. Clare**, Tom's second owner and father of Eva. Of the slaveowners in the novel, the most sympathetic character. St. Clare is complex, often sarcastic, with a ready wit. After a rocky courtship he marries a woman he grows to hold in contempt, though he is too polite to let it show. St. Clare recognizes the evil in chattel slavery, but is not willing to relinquish the wealth it brings him. After his daughter's death he becomes more sincere in his religious thoughts, and starts to read the Bible to Tom. He plans on finally taking action against slavery by freeing his slaves, but his good intentions ultimately come to nothing.

**Topsy**, A "ragamuffin" young slave girl. When asked if she knows who made her, she professes ignorance of both God and a mother, saying "I s'pect I growed. Don't think nobody never made me." She is transformed by Little Eva's love. During the early-to-mid 1900s, several doll manufacturers created Topsy and Topsy-type dolls. The phrase "growed like Topsy" (later "grew like Topsy"; now somewhat archaic) passed into the English language, originally with the specific meaning of unplanned growth, later sometimes just meaning enormous growth.

**Miss Ophelia**, is Augustine St. Clare's pious, hard-working, abolitionist cousin from Vermont. She displays the ambiguities towards African-Americans felt by many Northerners at the time. She argues against the institution of slavery yet, at least initially, feels repulsed by the slaves as individuals.

## Major themes

***"Uncle Tom's Cabin"*** is dominated by a single theme: the evil and immorality of slavery. She emphasizes the connections between these and the horrors of slavery. Stowe pushed home this theme consistently within the novel. She emphasizes for example, the destructive nature of slavery (such as when a white woman on the steamboat carrying Tom further south states, "The most dreadful part of slavery, to my mind, is its outrages of feelings and affections—the separating of families, for example.") In this manner Stowe showed the evil of slavery was how it forcibly separated families from each other.

Stowe saw motherhood as the "ethical and structural model for all of American life," and believed that only women had the moral authority to save the United States from the demon of slavery. She highlighted the moral power and sanctity of women. In characters like Eliza,

(Who escapes from slavery to save her young son(and eventually reunites her entire family.

Stowe believed women could save those around them from even the worst injustices. Stowe's novel "reaffirmed the importance of women's influence" and helped pave the way for the women's rights movement in the following decades.

## Style

***Uncle Tom's Cabin*** is written in the sentimental and melodramatic style , contemporary and common in 19th century novels and domestic fiction. Even though her depiction of the problems of slavery and having a man as the main character, she still set out to ***elicit certain strong feelings from her readers*** (such as making them cry at the death of Little Eva).

The power in this type of writing can be seen in the reaction of contemporary readers. Georgiana May, a friend of Stowe's, wrote a letter to the author stating that, "I was up last night long after one o'clock, reading and finishing ***Uncle Tom's Cabin***. I could not leave it any more than I could have left a dying child."

Another reader is described as obsessing on the book at all hours and having considered renaming her daughter Eva. The death of Little Eva affected a lot of people at that time, because in 1852 alone 300 baby girls in Boston were given that name.

Despite this positive reaction from readers, for decades literary critics dismissed the style found in ***Uncle Tom's Cabin*** and other sentimental novels because these books were written by women and so prominently featured, "women's sloppy emotions." One literary critic said that had the novel not been about slavery, "it would be just another sentimental novel,"

## Reaction to the novel

Upon publication, ***Uncle Tom's Cabin*** ignited a firestorm of protest from defenders of slavery (who created a number of books). It also ***outraged people in the American South***. The novel was also roundly criticized by slavery supporters.

A rebuttal soon appeared from northern born from pro-slavery writer, living at that time in the South with the publication of her own novel, "The Planter's Northern Bride' in which Hentz extolls the joys of slavery in the Old South as a natural institution.

Southern novelist William Gilmore Simms declared the work utterly false, while others called the novel criminal and slanderous. Reactions ranged from a bookseller in Mobile, Alabama who was forced to leave town for selling the novel to threatening letters sent to Stowe herself (including a package ***containing a slave's severed ear***). Some critics highlighted Stowe's lack of personal experience and knowledge of Southern life. They suggested due to any first-hand knowledge, that it led her to create inaccurate descriptions of the region. Their reasoning was based on the fact that ***she had never set foot on a Southern plantation***.

Stowe always said she based the characters of her book on stories ***she was told by runaway slaves in Cincinnati, Ohio,*** where Stowe resided. It had been stated that, "She observed firsthand several incidents which galvanized her to write (her) anti-slavery novel. Scenes she observed on the Ohio River, including seeing a husband and wife being sold apart, as well as newspaper and magazine accounts and interviews, contributed material to the emerging plot.

She responded in 1853 by publishing "***A Key to Uncle Tom's Cabin***," an attempt to document the veracity of the novel's depiction of slavery. In the book, Stowe discusses each of the major characters in ***Uncle Tom's Cabin*** and cited, "real life equivalents" to them while also mounting a more, "aggressive attack on slavery in the South than the novel itself had."The new novel, ***A Key to Uncle Tom's Cabin*** also became a best-seller.

Since then, many writers have credited this novel with focusing Northern anger at the injustices of slavery and the Fugitive Slave Law and helping to fuel the abolitionist movement. Union general and politician James Baird Weaver said that ***the book convinced him to become active in the abolitionist movement***.

***Uncle Tom's Cabin*** also created great interest in England. The first London edition appeared in May 1852, and sold 200,000 copies. Some of this interest was because of British antipathy to America.

## Note

Whilst Stowe claimed ***A Key to Uncle Tom's Cabin*** documented her previously consulted sources, she actually read many of the cited works only after the publication of her novel

## Southern Rebuttal to the Novel "Uncle Tom"

In response to Uncle Tom's Cabin, writers in the Southern United States produced a number of books to rebut Stowe's novel. This so-called Anti-Tom literature generally took a pro-slavery viewpoint, arguing that the issues of slavery as depicted in Stowe's book were overblown and incorrect. Among the most famous anti-Tom books are ***The Sword and the Distaff*** by William Gilmore Simms, ***Aunt Phillis's Cabin*** by Mary Henderson Eastman, and ***The Planter's Northern Bride*** by Caroline Lee Hentz, (Hentz had been a close personal friend of Stowe's when the two lived in Cincinnati.) Simms' book was published a few months after Stowe's novel and it contains a number of sections and discussions disputing Stowe's book and her view of slavery. Hentz's 1854 novel, was widely-read at the time. In it she offers a defense of slavery as seen through the eyes of a northern woman, the daughter of an abolitionist, no less,who marries a southern slave owner.

In the decade between the publication of Uncle Tom's Cabin and the start of the American Civil War, between twenty and thirty anti-Tom books were published. Among these novels are two books titled Uncle Tom's Cabin As It Is (one by W.L. Smith and the other by C.H. Wiley) and a book by John Pendleton Kennedy. Simms commenting at one point about the "Seemingly poetic justice of having the Northern woman (Stowe) answered by a Southern woman."

Another anti-"Uncle Tom book was aimed at a ***children's audience***, "Little Eva. ***The Flower of the South.***" by Philip J. Cozans.

# CAROLINE LEE HENTZ

## 1800-1856

Caroline Lee Whiting Hentz was a major literary figure who contributed to the advancement of women's fiction. She was best known for her literary contribution to the battle ***to defend slavery.*** Caroline was Alabama's first best-selling writer and one of the most popular women writers in antebellum America along with other southern novelists, such as Caroline Gilman and Augusta Jane Evans Wilson.

Born Caroline Lee Whiting on June 1, 1800, in Lancaster, Massachusetts, Hentz was the youngest of John and Orpah Whiting's eight children. At age 17, she began teaching at the Lancaster Common School. On September 30, 1824, Caroline married Nicholas Marcellus Hentz, a native of Metz, France, who had immigrated to America in 1816. An entomologist, novelist, and artist, Hentz was intellectually gifted but prone to depression and uncontrollable fits of jealousy. Not surprisingly, male jealousy would one day become a recurring theme in Hentz's fiction.

At the time of their marriage, Nicholas was teaching French at George Bancroft's Round Hill School in Northampton, Massachusetts.

After the family's initial move to Chapel Hill, North Carolina, in 1826, Caroline began writing a verse drama, ***De Lara, or The Moorish Bride,*** and edited the narrative of George Moses Horton, a slave. In 1830, the Hentzes moved to Covington, Kentucky, where Nicholas served as headmaster at a female academy and where Caroline completed ***De Lara***, which won a prize offered by Boston actor and manager William Pelby. *De Lara* was produced, to favorable reviews, at the Tremont Theater in Boston and the Arch Street Theater in Philadelphia. The following year, two more of her plays were produced, ***Constance of Werdenberg, or The Forest League,*** at the Park Theater in New York, and ***Lamorah, or the Western Wild,*** in Cincinnati, where the couple had moved in 1832 to oversee another school for girls.

Caroline joined a literary and social group in Cincinnati to which the future author Harriet Beecher Stowe also belonged. Twenty years later, Stowe's enormously popular antislavery novel, ***Uncle Tom's Cabin*** (1852), would inspire Hentz to defend slavery and the South by writing a pro-slavery novel, ***The Planter's Northern Bride*** (1854). While in Ohio, Hentz published her first novel, ***Lovell's Folly*** (1833), which included unfavorable portraits of recognizable northern citizens. Fearing libel charges, the publisher quickly withdrew the book from circulation.

In 1834, the Hentzes left Cincinnati following an incident in which Nicholas slapped a man who had sent Caroline a note after a party. Their often stormy marriage near collapse, the Hentzes moved to the frontier town of Florence, Alabama, where they established the Locust Dell Academy. During the next 14 years, the Hentzes operated girls' schools in Florence (1834-43), Tuscaloosa (1843-45), and Tuskegee (1845-48). Caroline continued to publish, but most of her time was spent assisting her husband at school, cooking meals for the students, and tending to her own children.

Although she was born in the North and lived in seven different states, Hentz spent 14 years in Alabama (1834-1848) with her husband and four children. Most of her fiction is set in the South, the region she adopted as home and fiercely defended from northern criticism. After her death, her sons Thaddeus and Charles served in the Confederate army, and after the war her oldest daughter, Julia, joined other southerners attempting to ***re-establish a slave-holding society*** in South America.

In 1848, the Hentzes moved to Columbus, Georgia, to open yet another school, but ***Nicholas's rapidly deteriorating mental state prompted them to close the school in 1849***. Two years later, the Hentzes moved to Marianna, Florida, ***where Caroline spent her remaining years caring for her husband*** and writing stories and novels at a feverish pace to support her family. She rapidly became one of America's most popular writers. Between 1850 and 1853, Hentz's books sold more than 93,000 copies, and as late as 1872, the Boston Public Library listed her as one of the three most popular authors of the day.

The popularity of Hentz's books can be attributed to her mastery in writing sentimental novels. The successful formula for these works centered on an innocent young woman, usually an orphan, who is pursued by an evil suitor through a variety of dangerous episodes until some handsome young man rescues her and joins her in a happy marriage. Other popular ingredients in the genre include narrow escapes, mistaken identity, romantic love and jealousy, religious sentiment and/or conversion, and an inspiring climb from rags to riches

Although much of the fiction of this genre has been criticized as overly sentimental, newer generations of feminist scholars have reevaluated the challenges it poses, however subtly, to male domination. In Hentz's *Eoline*, for example, the heroine rebels against her father by refusing to marry his choice of suitor, even though the penalty is the loss of her inheritance. In the end, Eoline marries the chosen suitor of her own free will. Hentz's work has also been examined for its promotion of Lost Cause ideology. ***The Planter's Northern Bride,*** for example, ***is a chilling rebuttal of Uncle Tom's Cabin.*** On its surface, the novel offers readers a sentimental marriage plot that covers a deeper theme defending the institution of slavery through the eloquent rhetoric of the main male character, planter Russell Moreland, and in many idyllic scenes of slave life.

The Hentzes did not live long to enjoy that success, however. When Nicholas's health grew worse, he moved to St. Andrews, Florida, to live with their daughter Julia. Caroline stayed in Marianna, traveling to St. Andrews occasionally to tend to her husband. ***She contracted pneumonia***

***and died on February 11, 1856. Her husband died nine months later, in November***. Both are buried in Marianna, Florida

## Selected Works

***Lamorah; or, the Western Wild*** (play, 1832)
***Constance of Werdenberg, or, The Forest League*** (play, 1832)
***Lovell's Folly*** (1833)
***De Lara; or, The Moorish Bride*** (1843)
***Human and Divine Philosophy: A Poem Written for the Erosophic Society of the University of Alabama*** (1844)
***Linda; or, The Young Pilot of the Belle Creole*** (1850)
***Rena; or, The Snow Bird*** (1851)
***Eoline; or, Magnolia Vale; or, The Heiress of Glenmore*** (1852)
***Marcus Warland; or, The Long Moss Spring*** (1852)
***The Banished Son and Other Stories of the Heart*** (1852)
***The Victim of Excitement, The Bosom Serpent, etc***. (1853)
***Wild Jack; or, The Stolen Child, and Other Stories*** (1853)
***The Planter's Northern Bri****de* (1854)
***Courtship and Marriage; or, The Joys and Sorrows of American Life*** (1856)
***The Lost Daughter and Other Stories of the Heart*** (1857)

'The Planter's Northern Bride' As ***an example of*** Caroline Lee Hentz's rebuttal to the popular 'northern' novel, "Uncle Tom's Cabin."

**THE PLANTER'S NORTHERN BRIDE**
**BY**
**MRS. CAROLINE LEE HENTZ.**

AUTHOR OF "LINDA," "RENA," "LOVE AFTER MARRIAGE," "ROBERT GRAHAM," "EOLINE," "COURTSHIP AND MARRIAGE," ETC.

***"I saw her, and I lov'd her—I sought her and I won;***
***A dozen pleasant summers, and more, since then have run***
***And half as many voices now prattling by her side,***
***Remind me of the autumn when she became my bride."***
—Thomas MacKellar

***"Nothing***
***shall assuage***
***Your love but marriage: for such is***
***The tying of two in wedlock, as is***
***The tuning of two lutes in one key: for***
***Striking the strings of the one, straws will stir***
***Upon the strings of the other; and in***
***Two minds linked in love, one cannot be***
***Delighted but the other rejoiceth."***
***—Lilly's Sappho***
***"Nothing"***

**Philadelphia:**
**T. B. PETERSON and BROTHERS,**
**306 CHESTNUT STREET.**

ENTERED; ***according to the Act of Congress, in the year 1854, by A. HART in the Clerk's Office of the District Court of the United States, in and for the Eastern District of Pennsylvania*** .COLLINS, PRINTER

**PREFACE**

IT was the intention of the author to have given this book to the world during the course of the past season, but unforeseen occurrences have prevented the accomplishment of her purpose. She no longer regrets the delay, as she believes it will meet a more cordial reception at the present time.

When individual or public feeling is too highly wrought on any subject, there must inevitably follow a reaction, and reason, recovering from the effects of transient inebriation, is ready to assert its original sovereignty. Not in the spirit of egotism, do we repeat what was said in the preface of a former work, that we were born at the North, and though destiny has removed us far from our native scenes, we cherish for them a sacred regard, an undying attachment. It cannot therefore be supposed that we are actuated by hostility or prejudice, in endeavouring to represent the unhappy consequences of that intolerant and fanatical spirit, whose fatal influence we so deeply deplore.

We believe that there are a host of noble, liberal minds, of warm, generous, candid hearts, at the North, that will bear us out in our views of Southern character, and that feel with us that our ***national*** honour is tarnished, when a portion of our country is held up to public disgrace and foreign insult, by those, too, whom every feeling of patriotism should lead to defend it from ignominy and shield it from dishonour. The hope that they will appreciate and do justice to our motives, has imparted enthusiasm to our feelings, and energy to our will, in the prosecution of our literary labour.

When we have seen the dark and horrible pictures drawn of slavery and exhibited to a gazing world, we have wondered if we were one of those favoured individuals to whom the fair side of life is ever turned, or whether we were created with a moral blindness, incapable of distinguishing its lights and shadows.

One thing is certain, and if we were on judicial oath we would repeat it, that during our residence in the South, we have never *witnessed* one scene of cruelty or oppression, never beheld a chain or a manacle, or the infliction of a punishment more severe than parental authority would be justified in applying to filial disobedience or transgression. This is not owing to our being placed in a limited sphere of observation, for we have seen and studied domestic, social, and plantation life, in Carolina, Alabama, Georgia, and Florida.

We have been admitted into close and familiar communion with numerous families in each of these States, not merely as a passing visiter, but as an indwelling guest, and we have never been pained by an inhuman exercise of authority, or a wanton abuse of power.

On the contrary, we have been touched and gratified by the exhibition of affectionate kindness and care on one side, and loyal and devoted attachment on the other. We have been especially struck with the cheerfulness and contentment of the slaves, and their usually elastic and buoyant spirits. From the abundant opportunities we have had of judging, we give it as our honest belief, that the Negroes of the South are the happiest ***labouring class*** on the face of the globe; even subtracting from their portion of enjoyment all that can truly be said of their trials and sufferings.

The fugitives who fly to the Northern States are no proof against the truth of this statement. They have most of them been made disaffected by the influence of others-- tempted by promises which are seldom fulfilled even in the garden of Eden, the seeds of discontent and rebellion were sown; surely we need not wonder that they sometimes take root in the beautiful groves of the South.

In the large cities we have heard of families who were cruel to their slaves, as well as unnaturally severe in the discipline of their children. (Are there no similar instances at the North?) But the indignant feeling which any known instance of inhumanity calls forth at the South, proves that they are not of common occurrence.

We have conversed a great deal with the coloured people, feeling the deepest interest in learning their own views of their peculiar situation, and we have almost invariably been delighted and affected by their humble devotion to their master's family, their child-like, affection reliance on their care and protection, and above all, with their genuine cheerfulness and contentment.

This very morning, since commencing these remarks, our sympathies have been strongly moved by the simple eloquence of a negro woman in speaking of her former master and mistress, who have been dead for many years.

"Oh!" said she, her eyes swimming with tears, and her voice choking with emotion, "I loved my master and mistress like my own soul. If I could have died in their stead, I would gladly done it. I would have gone into the grave and brought them up, if the Lord had let me do it. Oh! they were so good—so kind. All on us black folks would 'ave laid down our lives for 'em at any minute." Then you were happy?" we said; "you did not sigh to be free?"

"No, mistress, that I didn't. I was too well off for that. I wouldn't have left my master and mistress for all the freedom in the world. I'd left my own father and mother first. I loved 'em better than I done them. I loved their children too. Every one of 'em has been babies in my arms--and I loved 'em a heap better than I done my own, I want to stay with 'em as long as I live, and I know they will take care of me when I get too old to work."

These are her own words. We have not sought this simple instance of faithful and enduring love. It came to us as if in corroboration of our previous remarks, and we could not help recording it.

The history of Crissy and the circumstances of her abduction are true.
The character of Dr. Darley is drawn from life. Though death has now set the seal of eternity on his virtues, we would not violate the sanctity of private life by bringing his real name before the public. Should those he loved best on earth recognise the lineaments we have attempted to draw, may they accept this imperfect tribute to his exalted worth, his brilliant and commanding talents, as well as his pure and genuine philanthropy.

Many of the circumstance we have recorded in these pages are founded on truth. The plot of the insurrection, the manner in which it was instigated and detected, and the brief history of Nat, the giant, with his domestication in a Northern family, are literally true.If any one should think the affection manifested by the slaves of Moreland for their master is too highly coloured, we would refer them to the sketch of Thomas Jefferson's arrival at Monticello on his return from Paris, after an absence of five years. It is from the pen of his daughter, and no one will doubt its authenticity.

The negroes discovered the approach of the carriage as soon as it reached Shadwell, and such a scene I never witnessed in my life. They collected in crowds around it, and almost drew it up the mountain by hand. The shouting, &c., had been sufficiently obstreperous before, but the moment the carriage arrived on the top it reached the climax. When the door of the carriage was opened, they received him in their arms and bore him into the house, crowding around, kissing his hands and feet, some blubbering and crying, others laughing. It appeared impossible to satisfy their eyes, or their anxiety to touch, and even to kiss the very earth that bore him.

These were the first ebullitions of joy for his return, after a long absence, which they would of course feel; but it is perhaps not out of place to add here, that they were at all times very devoted in their attachment to their master. They believed him to be one of the greatest, and they knew him to be one of the best of men, and kindest of masters. They spoke to him freely, and applied confidingly to him in all their difficulties and distresses; and he watched over them in sickness and health; interested himself in all their concerns; advising them, and showing esteem and confidence in the good, and indulgence to all."

We can add nothing to this simple, pathetic description. Monticello is hallowed ground, and the testimony that proceeds from its venerated retreat should be listened to with respect and confidence. The same accents might be heard from Mount Vernon's august shades, where the grave of Washington has been bedewed by the tears of the grateful African. But we have done. If we fail to accomplish the purpose for which we have written, we shall at least have the consolation of knowing that our motives are disinterested, and our aim patriotic and true.
Should no Northern heart respond to our earnest appeal, we trust the voice of the South will answer to our own, not in a faint, cold, dying echo, but in a full, spontaneous strain, whose reverberations shall reach to the green hills and granite cliffs of New England's "rock-bound coast."

## CHAPTER I

MR. MORELAND, a Southern planter, was travelling through the New England States in the bright season of a Northern spring. Business with some of the merchant princes of Boston had brought him to the North; but a desire to become familiar with the beautiful surroundings of the metropolis induced him to linger long after it was transacted, to gratify the taste and curiosity of an intelligent and liberal mind. He was rich and independent, had leisure as well as wealth at his command, and there was something in the deep green fields and clear blue waters of New England that gave a freshness, and brightness, and elasticity to his spirits, wanting in his milder, sunnier latitude.

He found himself one Saturday night in a sweet country village, whose boundaries were marked by the most luxuriant shubbery and trees, in the midst of which a thousand silver rills were gushing. He was pleased with the prospect of passing the ensuing Sunday in a valley so serene and quiet, that it seemed as if Nature enjoyed in its shades the repose of an eternal Sabbath. The inn where he stopped was a neat, orderly place, and though the landlord impressed him, at first, as a hard, repulsive looking man, with a dark, Indian face, and large, iron-bound frame, he found him ready to perform all the duties of a host. Requesting to be shown to a private apartment, he ordered Albert, a young mulatto who accompanied him on his journey, to follow him with his valise.

Albert was a handsome, golden-skinned youth, with shining black hair and eyes, dressed very nearly as genteelly as his master, and who generally attracted more attention on their Northern tour. Accustomed to wait on his master and listen to the conversation of refined and educated gentlemen, he had very little of the dialect of the negro, and those familiar with the almost unintelligible jargon which delineators of the sable character put into their lips, could not but be astonished at the propriety of his language and pronunciation.

When Mr. Moreland started on his journey to the North, his friends endeavoured to dissuade him from taking a servant with him, as he would incur the danger of losing him among the granite hills to which he was bound:—they especially warned him of the risk of taking Albert, whose superior intelligence and cultivation would render him more accessible to the arguments which would probably be brought forward to lure him from his allegiance.

"I defy all the eloquence of the North to induce Albert to leave me," exclaimed Mr. Moreland. "Let them do it if they can. Albert," he said, calling the boy to him, who was busily employed in brushing and polishing his master's boots, with a friction quick enough to create sparkles of light. "Albert,--I am going to the North--would you like to go with me?"

"To be sure I would, master, I would like to go anywhere in the world with you." "You know the people are all free at the North, Albert " "Yes, master.

"And when you are there, they will very likely try to persuade you that you are free too, and tell you it is your duty to run away from me, and set up for a gentleman yourself. What do you think of all this?"

Albert suspended his brush in the air, drew up his left shoulder with a significant shrug, darted an oblique glance at his master from his bright black eyes, and then renewed his friction with accelerated velocity.

"Well, my boy, you have not answered me," cried Mr. Moreland, in a careless, yet interested manner, peculiar to himself.

"Why, you see, Mars. Russell (when he addressed his master by his Christian name, he always abbreviated his title in this manner, though when the name was omitted he uttered the title in all its dignity),--"you see, Mars. Russell,"--here the mulatto slipped the boot from his arm, placed it on the floor, and still retaining the brush in his right hand, folded his arms across his breast, and spoke deliberately and earnestly,—"they couldn't come round this boy with that story; I've heard it often enough already; I ain't afraid of anything they can say and do, to get me away from you as long as you want me to stay with you. But if you are afraid to trust me, master, that's another thing. You'd better leave me, if you think I'd be mean enough to run away."

***First Frontispiece Image***

MR. AND MRS. MORELAND AND ALBERT
Philadelphia: T. B. Peterson, c1854

"Well said, Albert!" exclaimed Mr. Moreland, laughing at the air of injured honour and conscious self-appreciation he assumed; "I do trust you, and shall surely take you with me; you can make yourself very amusing to the people, by telling them of your home frolics, such as being chained, handcuffed, scourged, flayed, and burned alive, and all those little trifles they are so much interested in."

"Oh! master, I wish I may find everybody as well off as I am. If there's no lies told on you but what I tell, you'll be mighty safe, I know. Ever since Miss Claudia"—"Enough," cried Mr. Moreland, hastily interrupting him. He had breathed a name which evidently awakened painful recollections, for his sunshiny countenance became suddenly dark and cold. Albert, who seemed familiar with his master's varying moods, respectfully resumed his occupation, while Mr. Moreland took up his hat and plunged into the soft, balmy atmosphere of a Southern spring morning.

It is not our intention to go back and relate the past history of Mr. Moreland. It will be gathered in the midst of unfolding events, at least all that is necessary for the interest of our story. We will therefore return to the white-walled inn of the fair New England village, where our traveller was seated, enjoying the long, dewy twilight of the new region in which he was making a temporary rest.

The sun had gone down, but the glow of his parting smile lingered on the landscape and reddened the stream that gleamed and flashed through the distant shrubbery. Not far from the inn, on a gradual eminence, rose the village church, whose tall spire, surmounted by a horizontal vane, reposed on the golden clouds of sunset, resembling the crucifix of some gorgeous cathedral.

This edifice was situated far back from the road, surrounded by a common of the richest green, in the centre of which rose the swelling mound, consecrated by the house of God. Some very handsome buildings were seen at regular intervals, on either side of the road, among which the court-house stood conspicuous, with its freestone-coloured wall and lofty cupola.

There was something in the aspect of that church, with its heaven-ascending spire, whose glory-crown of lingering day-beams glittered with a kind of celestial splendour, reminding him of the halo which encircles the brows of saints; something in the deep tranquillity of the hour, the soft, hazy, undulating outline of the distant horizon, the swaying motion of the tall poplars that margined the street far as his eye could reach, and through whose darkening vista a solitary figure gradually lessened on the eye, that solemnized and even saddened the spirits of our traveller.

The remembrances of early youth and opening manhood pressed upon him with suddenly awakened force. Hopes, on which so sad and awful a blight had fallen, raised themselves like faded flowers sprinkled with dew, and mocked him with their visionary bloom. In the excitement of travelling, the realities of business, the frequent collision of interests, the championship of oft invaded rights, he had lost much of that morbidness of feeling and restlessness of character, which, being more accidental than inherent, would naturally yield to the force of circumstances counter to those in which they were born. But at the close of any arbitrary division of time, such as the last day of the week or the year, the mind is disposed to deeper meditation, and the mental burden, whose weight has been equipoised by worldly six-day cares, rolls back upon the mind with leaden oppression.

Moreland had too great a respect for the institutions of religion, too deep an inner sense of its power, to think of continuing his journey on the Sabbath, and he was glad that the chamber which he occupied looked out upon that serene landscape, and that the morning shadow of the lofty church-spire would be thrown across his window.

It seemed to him he had seen this valley before, with its beautiful green, grassy slopes, its sunset-gilded church, and dark poplar avenue. And it seemed to him also, that he had seen a fair maiden form gliding through the central aisle of that temple, in robes of virgin white, and soft, down-bending eyes of dark brown lustre, and brow of moonlight calmness.

It was one of those dim reminiscences, those vague, dream-like consciousnesses of a previous existence, which every being of poetic temperament is sometimes aware of, and though they come, faint shadows of a far-off world, quick and vanishing as lightning, they nevertheless leave certain traces of their presence, "trails of glory," as a great poet has called them, proceeding from the spirit's home.

While he sat leaning in silence against the window frame, the bell of the church began to toll slowly and solemnly, and as the sounds rolled heavily and gloomily along, then reverberated and vibrated with melancholy prolongation, sending out a sad, dying echo, followed by another majestic, startling peal, he wondered to hear such a funeral knell at that twilight hour, and looked up the shadowy line of poplars for the dark procession leading to the grave.

Nothing was seen, however, and nothing heard but those monotonous, heavy, mournful peals, which seemed to sweep by him with the flaps of the raven's wings. Twenty times the bell tolled, and then all was still. "What means the tolling of the bell?" asked he of the landlord, who was walking beneath the window. "Is there a funeral at this late hour? A young woman has just died," replied the landlord. "They are tolling her age. It is a custom of our village."

Moreland drew back with a shudder, ***just twenty***. That was ***her*** age. ***She*** had not died, and yet the death-bell might well ring a deeper knell over her than the being who had just departed. In the grave the remembrance of the bitterest wrongs are buried, and the most vindictive cease to thirst for vengeance. Moreland was glad when a summons to supper turned his thoughts into a different channel.

There might have been a dozen men seated around the table, some whose dress and manners proclaimed that they were gentlemen, others evidently of a coarser grain. They all looked up at the entrance of Moreland, who, with a bow, such as the courteous stranger is always ready to make, took his seat, while Albert placed himself behind his master's chair.

"Take a seat," said Mr. Grimby, the landlord, looking at Albert. "There's one by the gentleman, plenty of room for us all." "My boy will wait," cried Mr. Moreland with unconscious haughtiness, while his pale cheek visibly reddened. "I would thank you to leave the arrangement of such things to myself." "No offence, I hope, sir," rejoined Mr. Grimby. "We look ***upon everybody here as free and equal.*** This is a free country, and when folks come among us we don't see why they can't conform to our ways of thinking. There's a proverb that says—'when you're with the Romans, it's best to do as the Romans do.' "

"Am I to understand," said Mr. Moreland, fixing his eye deliberately on his Indian-visaged host, "that you wish my servant to sit down with yourself and these gentlemen?" "To be sure I do," replied the landlord, winking his small black eye knowingly at his left-hand neighbour. "I don't see why he isn't as good as the rest of us. I'm an enemy to all distinctions myself, and I'd like to bring everybody round to my opinion."

"Albert!" cried his master, "obey the landlord's wishes. ***I*** want no supper; take my seat and see that you are well attended to." "Mars. Russell," said the mulatto, in a confused and deprecating tone. "Do as I tell you," exclaimed Mr. Moreland, in a tone of authority, which, though tempered by kindness, Albert understood too well to resist. As Moreland passed from the room, a gentleman, with a very preposessing countenance and address, who was seated on the opposite side of the table, rose and followed him.

"I am sorry you have had so poor a specimen of Northern politeness," said the gentleman, accosting Moreland, with a slight embarrassment of manner. "I trust you do not think we all endorse such sentiments." "I certainly must make you an exception, sir," replied Moreland, holding out his hand with involuntary frankness; "but I fear there are but very few.

This is, however, the first direct attack I have received, and I hardly knew in what way to meet it. I have too much self-respect to place myself on a level with a man so infinitely my inferior. That he intended to insult me, I know by his manner. He knows our customs at home, and that nothing could be done in more positive violation of them than his unwarrantable proposition."

They had walked out in the open air while they were speaking, and continued their walk through the poplar avenue, through whose stiff and stately branches the first stars of evening were beginning to glisten. "I should think you would fear the effect of these things on your servant," said the gentleman,—"that it would make him insolent and rebellious. Pardon me, sir, but I think you were rather imprudent in bringing him with you, and exposing him to the influences which must meet him on every side. You will not be surprised, after the instance which has just occurred, when I tell you, that, in this village, you are in the very hot-bed of fanaticism; and that a Southern planter, accompanied by his slave, can meet but little sympathy, consideration, or toleration; I fear there will be strong efforts made to induce your boy to leave you."

"I fear nothing of that kind," answered Moreland. "If they can bribe him from me, let him go. I brought him far less to minister to my wants than to test his fidelity and affection. I believe them proof against any temptation or assault; if I am deceived I wish to know it, though the pang would be as severe as if my own brother should lift his hand against me."

"Indeed!—I did not imagine that the feelings were ever so deeply interested. While I respect your rights, and resent any un-gentlemanlike infringement of them, as in the case of our landlord, I cannot conceive how beings, who are ranked as goods and chattels, things of bargain and traffic, can ever fill the place of a friend or brother in the heart."

"Nevertheless, I assure you, that next to our own kindred, we look upon our slaves as our best friends."

As they came out of the avenue into the open street, they perceived the figure of a woman, walking with slow steps before them, bearing a large bundle under her arm; she paused several times, as if to recover breath, and once she stopped and leaned against the fence, while a dry, hollow cough rent her frame.

"Nancy," said the gentleman, "is that you? - you should not be out in the night air. The woman turned round, and the starlight fell on a pale and wasted face. I can't help it," she answered,--"I can't hold out any longer,—I can't work any more;—I ain't strong enough to do a single chore now; and Mr. Grimby says he hadn't got any room for me to lay by in. My wages stopped three weeks ago. He says there's no use in my hanging on any longer, for I'll never be good for anything any more."

"Where are you going now?" said the gentleman. "Home!" was the reply, in a tone of deep and hopeless despondency,—"Home, to my poor old mother. I've supported her by my wages ever since I've been hired out; that's the reason I haven't laid up any. God knows—" Here she stopped, for her words were evidently choked by an awful realization of the irremediable misery of her condition. Moreland listened with eager interest. His compassion was awakened, and so were other feelings. Here was a problem he earnestly desired to solve, and he determined to avail himself of the opportunity thrown in his path.

"How far is your home from here?" he asked. "About three-quarters of a mile." "Give me your bundle—I'll carry it for you, you are too feeble; nay, I insist upon it." Taking the bundle from the reluctant hand of the poor woman, he swung it lightly upward and poised it on his left shoulder. His companion turned with a look of unfeigned surprise towards the elegant and evidently high-bred stranger, thus courteously relieving poverty and weakness of an oppressive burden.

"Suffer me to assist you," said he. "You must be very unaccustomed to services of this kind; I ought to have anticipated you." "I am not accustomed to do such things for myself," answered Moreland, "because there is no occasion; but it only makes me more willing to do them for others. You look upon us as very self-indulging beings, do you not?"

"We think your institutions calculated to promote the growth of self-indulgence and selfishness. The virtues that resist their opposing influences must have more than common vitality." We, who know the full length and breadth of our responsibilities, have less time than any other men for self-indulgence. We feel that life is too short for the performance of our duties, made doubly arduous and irksome by the misapprehension and prejudice of those who ought to know us better and judge us more justly and kindly. My good woman, do we walk too fast?"

"Oh, no, sir. I so long to get home, but I am so ashamed to have you carry that bundle." He had forgotten the encumbrance in studying the domestic problem, presented to him for solution. Here was a poor young woman, entirely dependent on her daily labour for the support of herself and aged mother, incapacitated by sickness from ministering to their necessities, thrown back upon her home, without the means of subsistence: in prospective, a death of lingering torture for herself, for her mother a life of destitution or a shelter in the almshouse. For every comfort, for the bare necessaries of life, they must depend upon the compassion of the public; the attendance of a physician must be the work of charity, their existence a burden on others.

She had probably been a faithful labourer in her employer's family, while health and strength lasted. He was an honest man in the common acceptation of the word, and had doled out her weekly wages as long as they were earned; but he was not rich, he had no superfluous gold, and could not afford to pay to her what was due to her stronger and more healthy successor; he could not afford to give her even the room which was required by another.

What could she do but go to her desolate home and die? She could not murmur. She had no claim on the affection of the man in whose service she had been employed. She had lived with him in the capacity of a hireling, and he, satisfied that he paid her the utmost farthing which justice required, dismissed her, without incurring the censure of unkindness or injustice. We ought to add, without deserving it. There were others far more able than himself to take care of her, and a home provided by the parish for every unsheltered head.Moreland, whose moral perceptions were rendered very acute by observation, drew a contrast in his own mind, between the Northern and Southern labourer, when reduced to a state of sickness and dependence.

He brought his own experience in comparison with the lesson of the present hour, and thought that the sick and dying negro, retained under his master's roof, kindly nursed and ministered unto, with no sad, anxious lookings forward into the morrow for the supply of nature's wants, no fears of being cast into the pauper's home, or of being made a member of that unhappy family, consecrated by no head, hallowed by no domestic relationship, had in contrast a far happier lot. In the latter case there was no sickness, without its most horrible concomitant, poverty, without the harrowing circumstances connected with public charity, or the capricious influence of private compassion.

It is true, the nominal bondage of the slave was wanting, but there was the bondage of poverty, whose iron chains are heard clanking in every region of God's earth, whose dark links are wrought in the forge of human suffering, eating slowly into the quivering flesh, till they reach and dry up the life-blood of the heart. It has often been said that there need be no such thing as poverty in this free and happy land; that here it is only the offspring of vice and intemperance; that the avenues of wealth and distinction are open to all. and that all who choose may arrive at the golden portals of success and honour, and enter boldly in.

Whether this be true or not, let the thousand toiling operatives of the Northern manufactories tell; let the poor, starving seamstresses, whose pallid faces mingle their chill, wintry gleams with the summer glow and splendour of the Northern cities, tell; let the free negroes, congregated in the suburbs of some of our modern Babylons, lured from their homes by hopes based on sand, without forethought, experience, or employment, without sympathy, influence, or caste, let them also tell.

When Moreland reached the low, dark-walled cottage which Nancy pointed out as her home, he gave her back her bundle, and at the same time slipped a bill into her hand, of whose amount she could not be aware. But she knew by the soft, yielding paper the nature of the gift, and something whispered her that it was no niggard boon. "Oh, sir," she cried, "you are too good. God bless you, sir, over and over again!"

She stood in the doorway of the little cabin, and the dull light within played luridly on her sharpened and emaciated features. Her large black eyes were burning with consumption's wasting fires, and a deep red, central spot in each concave cheek, like the flame of the magic cauldron, was fed with blood alone. Large tears were now sparkling in those glowing flame-spots, but they did not extinguish their wasting brightness.

"Poor creature!" thought Moreland. "Her day of toil is indeed over. There is nothing left for her but to endure and to die. She has learned to ***labour***, she must now learn to ***wait***." As he turned from the door, resolving to call again before he left the village, he saw his companion step back and speak to her, extending his hand at the same time. Perceiving that he was actuated by the Christian spirit, which does not wish the left hand to know what the right hand doeth, he walked slowly on, through an atmosphere perfumed by the delicious but oppressive fragrance of the blossoming lilacs, that lent to this obscure habitation a certain poetic charm.

During their walk back to the inn, he became more and more pleased with his new acquaintance, whose name he ascertained was Brooks, by profession an architect of bridges. He was not a resident of the village, but was now engaged in erecting a central bridge over the river that divided the village from the main body of the town. As his interests were not identified with the place or the people, his opinions were received by Moreland with more faith and confidence than if they issued from the lips of a native inhabitant.

When they returned to the inn, they found Albert waiting at the door, with a countenance of mingled vexation and triumph. The landlord and several other men were standing near him, and had evidently been engaged in earnest conversation. The sudden cessation of this, on the approach of Mr. Moreland, proved that he had been the subject of it, and from the manner in which they drew back as he entered the passage, he imagined their remarks were not of the most flattering nature.

"Well, Albert, my boy," said he, when they were alone in his chamber, "I hope you relished your supper." "Please, Mars. Russell, don't do that again. I made 'em wait on me this time, but it don't seem right. Besides, I don't feel om an equality with ‘em, no way, They are no gentlemen.” Moreland laughed. "What were they talking to you about so earnestly as I entered?" asked he. "About how you treated me and the rest of us. Why, Mars. Russell, ***they don't know nothing about us.***

They want to know if we don't wear chains at home and manacles about our wrists. One asked if you didn't give us fodder to eat. Another wanted to strip off my coat, to see if my back wa'n't all covered with scars. I wish you'd heard what I told 'em. Master, I wish you'd heard the way I give it to 'em." "I have no doubt you did me justice, Albert. My feelings are not in the least wounded, though my sense of justice is pained. Why, I should think the sight of your round, sleek cheeks, and sound, active limbs would be the best argument in my favour. They must believe you thrive wonderfully on fodder."

What you think one of 'em said, Mars. Russell? They say you fatten me up, you dress me up, and carry me 'bout as a show-boy, to make folks think you treat us all well, but that the niggers at home are treated worse than dogs or cattle, a heap worse. I tell 'em it's all one big lie. I tell 'em you're the best—"Never mind, Albert. That will do. I want to think-"

Albert never ventured to intrude on his master's thinking moments, and, turning away in respectful silence, he soon stretched himself on the carpet and sunk in a profound sleep. In the mean time Moreland waded through a deep current of thought that swelled as it rolled, and oft times it was turbid and foaming, and sometimes it seemed of icy chillness. He was a man of strong intellect and strong passions; but the latter, being under the control of principle, gave force and energy and warmth to a character which, if unrestrained, they would have defaced and laid waste.

He was a searcher after truth, and felt ready and brave enough to plunge into the cold abyss, where it is said to be hidden, or to encounter the fires of persecution, the thorns of prejudice, to hazard everything, to suffer everything, rather than relinquish the hope of attaining it. He pondered much on the condition of mankind, its inequalities and wrongs. He thought of the poor and subservient in other lands, and compared them with our own.

He thought of the groaning serfs of Russia; the starving sons of Ireland; the squalid operatives of England, its dark, subterranean workshops, sunless abodes of want, misery, and sin, its toiling millions, doomed to drain their hearts' best blood to add to the splendors and luxuries of royalty and rank; of the free hirelings of the North, who, as a ***class***, travail in discontent and repining, anxious to throw off the yoke of servitude, sighing for an equality which exists only in name; and then he turned his thoughts homeward, to the enslaved children of Africa, and, taking them as a ***class***, as a ***distinct race*** of beings, he came to the irresistible conclusion, that they were the happiest ***subservient*** race that were found on the face of the globe.

He did not seek to disguise to himself the evils which were inseparably connected with their condition, or that man too oft abused the power he owned; but in view of all this, in view of the great, commanding truth, that wherever civilized man exists, there is the dividing line of the high and the low, the rich and the poor, the thinking and the laboring, in view of the God-proclaimed fact that "all Creation toileth and groaneth together," and that labour and suffering are the solemn sacraments of life, he believed that the slaves of the South were blest beyond the pallid slaves of Europe, or the anxious, care-worn labourers of the North.

With this conviction he fell asleep, and in his dreams he still tried to unravel the mystery of life, and to reconcile its inequalities with the justice and mercy of an omnipotent God.

**END OF CHAPTER ONE**

## EULALIA AND THE NIGHTMARE

**The Planter's Northern Bride**
Philadelphia: T. B. Peterson, 1854

**CLAUDIA AND EULALIA**

**The Planter's Northern Bride**
Philadelphia: T. B. Peterson, 1854

# SARAH T. BOLTON

**Dec. 18, 1814 - Aug. 4, 1893**

Sarah Tittle Barrett Bolton (Dec. 18, 1814 - Aug. 4, 1893) was born in Newport, Kentucky.The daughter of Jonathan Belcher and the oldest of six children. In her early years she lived in a rural area, just outside of Vernon, Indiana. She spent most of her time exploring its wilderness this influence was reflected in her earlier poetry, and is evident in her poem "***Our Pioneers***" part of a collection from 'Songs of a life-time'

*OUR PIONEERS* **(*Excerpt*)**

Once more, O friends, in life we meet
Where Oakland's forest cool and green
Spreads summer grass beneath our feet,
Above our heads a leafy screen,
And bright-winged birds all day long
Pour out their happiness in song.

The poem goes on to explain the hardships and sacrifices that the pioneers of Indiana had to go through. She goes into detail how everyone helped their neighbor, went to church, and then later started to build up a community. She plots out how Indiana went from a wilderness to a society:

Life in the wilderness went slow,
There were no famous lectures then,
No circus with its royal show
Of tinseled women, juggling men;
No acrobats, no grand trapeze,
In these wild woods, in those days

Those olden times have passed away,
And in the clearing by the wood,
Fair architecture builds, to-day,
Proud mansions where the cabin stood,
And cities lift their dooms and spires
Where hunters struck their lone camp-fires

Sarah Bolton was raised in rural Indiana. The landscape changed over time, as settlers clear the land from forests that had been cleared to a land of fields and farms. This change was witnessed by her and had impacted her style of writing. At the age of nine, her father sold their farmhouse and moved to Madison. She appears to have been a competent student and she enjoyed writing. Before the age of fourteen she had composed items and they appeared regularly in her hometown newspaper, the Madison Banner. She then contributed material further afield to newspapers in Cincinatti. In this period she wrote the poems, "Our Pioneers" and "A Pioneer Grandmother".

She married Nathaniel Bolton, (They had known each other for over three years, since she had first contributed poetry to the newspaper.) A year later they moved to live in Indianapolis where her husband was hired as editor of the Indiana Democrat. (He later became an owner of a tavern.)

***MADISON***

Home of my long-gone childhood, still thou art
Of living memory, love and life a part-
No classic city in a classic land,
However stately, beautiful and grand,
Could ever in my fond affection be
What thou hast been, what thou art to me.
I never hear thy name but thought goes back,
Along the path that bore my childhood's track.

Again I climb the summit of thy hills-
Hear the sweet rhythmic music of thy rills,
And learn the story that the passing breeze
Tells, of its wanderings, to the ancient trees.
I find the rock-ribbed gorge, the mossy dell,
Where hairbells ring and fairy people dwell;
And, when a beechen bough is rudely stirred,
I hear a dryad whispering some fond word,
Of tender warning, to the trembling leaves,
That answer, murmuring, like a heart that grieves.

The poem continues on with more fond recollections, and other description of how she spent her time in Madison as a little girl.

In her poem "***Indiana,***" was included in "***The Life and Poems of Sarah T. Bolton***," it reflects her feelings and pride and her remembrance of the state she grew up in as a child:

***INDIANA***

Though many laud Italia's clime,
And call Helvetia's land sublime,
Tell Gallia's praise in prose and rhyme,
And worship old Hispania:
The winds of Heaven never spanned
The borders of a better land
Than our own Indiana.

Encrowned with forests grand and old,
Enthroned on mineral wealth untold,
Coining her soil to yellow gold,
Through labor's great arcana,
She fosters commerce, science, art,
With willing hands and generous heart,
And sends to many a foreign mart
Products of Indiana.
Where late the birchen wigwam stood,
Or Indiana braves their game pursued,
And Indian maids were won and wooed,
By light of soft Diana,
Fair cities as by magic rise,
With church towers pointing to the skies,
And school's that charm the world's wide eyes
To fair young Indiana.

And, where some fifty years ago,
The settler's wagon lumbered slow
Through mud, and mire, and frozen snow,
O'er hillside and savannah,
The steam car, with its fiery eyes,
Like some mad demon pants and flies,
Startling the echoes with its cries
Throughout all Indiana.

Not to old realms, with palace piles
And crowned kings—nor sea-girt isles,
Wherein perpetual summer smiles
On bread-fruit and banana,
could we, in word or thought compare,
The free domain, the balmy air,
The silver streams and valleys fair,
Of genial Indiana.
With kindly word and friendly hand
She welcomes sons of every land.
From Hammerfest to Samarcand.
From India to Briannia;
And many a toile, sore opprest
In olden lands, has found his quest—
A happy homestead—on the breast
Of fruitful Indiana.
She gives the hungry stranger bread;
Her helpless poor are clothed and fed
As freely as the Father spread
The feast of mystic manna,
The sick in body, wrecked in mind,
A free and safe asylum find
In generous Indiana.
Her genele mothers, pure and good,
In stately homes of cabine rude,
Are types of noble womanhood;
Her girls are sweet and cannie;
her sons, among the bravest, brave,
Call no man master, no man slave—
Holding the heritage God gave.

While her husband was busy running the tavern, she was both a housekeeper and cook, at the same time she operated a large dairy farm. During this period she wrote her first collection of poems, “Paddle Your Own Canoe.”

Throughout the 1840s and 50s Mrs. Bolton was considered the unofficial poet laureate of Indiana. She continued to write poetry and be published in newspapers and home journals. Her writings and participation in public affairs made her a prominent figure in Indiana.

She was interested in various reforms, and was an active aid to Robert Dale Owen in his effort to secure property rights for women in the constitutional convention of 1850. She was an ardent democrat and champion of freedom, full of patriotism and faith in the country's future.

Her life, however, was shaped by her husband's fortunes He died in 1858. Later he became a state librarian, then clerk of a United States Senate. About five years after his death, she married Judge Addison Reese on September 15th 1863 in Keokuk, Iowa. For the next two years lived with him at his home in Canton, Mo. The climate there was not favorable to her health, and she returned to Indianapolis, where she made her home until her death..

During the 1840s and 50s, she was considered the unofficial poet laureate of Indiana. She continued to write poetry and be published in newspapers and home journals. Later, Mr. Bolton became a U.S. councilman in Geneva, Switzerland, where he died. Five years after her husband's death, Sarah Bolton remarried.

Later in her life she traveled a good deal in Europe and out west in the United States. She still missed her home state of Indiana. Hearkening back to those days she composed several poems about the simple rural life she had to leave so may years earlier. Her poems contained the contemporary style of maudlin sentimentality, also moral and religious messages which were welcomed by the fireside magazine' readers of that era.

'Paddle Your Own Canoe' and a few others had wide popularity. Poems appeared in 1865. Later a collection of her writings together with a description of her career was published in 1880 in 'The Life and Poems of Sarah T. Bolton.' A volume of selections, 'Songs of a life time,' edited by John Clark Ridpath, was published in 1892.

## Sources

Ladies' Repository, Feb. 1852, pp. 69-73;
Wm.W. Woollen, Biog, and Hist. Sketches of Early Indiana, 1883).